"Depression cares nothing for .... geous and groundbreaking memoir, Nana-Ama Danquah tells the story of her struggles as a Black woman living with the anguish of mental illness. Her prose is lyrical and its message is profound; this narrative will provide comfort, wisdom, and dignity to people of all colors who face the demons she has long grappled with."

—Imbolo Mbue, author of *How Beautiful We Were*

"Personal and political, tender and powerful, *Willow Weep for Me* speaks to readers from the timeless landscape of human emotion about the ordinary and extraordinary challenges of living thoughtfully and compassionately in the world. This book is needed as urgently today as it was when it was first released twenty-five years ago. Its enduring potency is a testament to Danquah's unnerving ability to get at the heart of an experience that is as disturbing as it is universal."

—Emily Bernard, author of *Black Is the Body*

"I found *Willow Weep for Me* at a time when I needed it desperately. Nana-Ama Danquah's memoir is a work of profound beauty and power, illuminating a path to self-knowledge and reclamation."

—Nadia Owusu, author of *Aftershocks*

"Absorbing and inspirational. . . . A vividly textured flower of a memoir that will surely stand as one of the finest to come along in years." —*Washington Post Book World*

"[*Willow Weep for Me*] is no easy read. But, before I realize, I am deep inside its story, inside its sadness, its pain. I am lured by [Nana-Ama Danquah's] seductive, lyrical, descriptive prose. . . . Danquah and the other black women, whose lives she charts in her book, have decided that they can't wait to be rescued. . . . *Willow Weep for Me* is a powerful lens."

—*Washington Times*

"Danquah has written an important and moving memoir. She describes beautifully her experiences with depression and provides a unique and compelling account of her life. *Willow Weep for Me* is not only a lovely book, it is a powerful one."

—Kay Redfield Jamison, author of *An Unquiet Mind*

"*Willow Weep for Me* is a tremendous contribution to the health of black women; and, also, a tremendous gift to all of us and to our understanding of depression, and its pervasiveness throughout our society."

—David Satcher, MD, PhD,
16th Surgeon General of the United States

"In *Willow Weep for Me*, Danquah has opened up one of our silenced spaces. Her courage and honesty strengthen. Her words heal."   —Junot Díaz, author of *This Is How You Lose Her*

"*Willow Weep for Me* is both a moving personal memoir and a superb account of one woman's brave struggle against depression. Beautifully written, painfully blunt at times, this book will only grow in stature over the years."

—Tim O'Brien, author of *The Things They Carried*

"At long last, a book that focuses on the emotional anguish and despair experienced by countless black women. The vulnerability exposed in *Willow Weep for Me* is necessary, right, and true. This book will do much to transform society's image of black women as sturdy bridges to everyone's healing except their own."

—Evelyn C. White, editor of *The Black Women's Health Book*

"*Willow Weep for Me* leads us into the tiny, suffocating closet that is depression and locks the door. I applaud Danquah for the courage it took to refuse silence. As African Americans, we often believe hiding our 'dirty laundry'—our humanity and fallibility—is an essential means of survival. But Danquah shows us it's a dangerous ruse. Not a glossed-over portrait of easy healing, this is a riveting and necessarily disturbing book."   —Lisa Jones, author of *Bulletproof Diva*

"Danquah writes here with insight and searing clarity about the circumstances of race, gender, and culture which underlie her depression. What she achieves is an artful, intimate memoir which breaks the deafening silence that continues to shroud black women and depression. This book is a true and healing mirror for the many, many women who dismiss their own debilitating symptoms of depression and instead wish in silence that tomorrow will be a better day."

—Rebecca Walker, author of *Black, White, and Jewish*

"A very important text. Danquah has shed light on a serious problem within the African American community. Her memoir might just save a few lives."

—E. Ethelbert Miller, author of *If God Invented Baseball*

Willow Weep *for* Me

WILLOW WEEP
for ME

A Black Woman's Journey

Through Depression

A MEMOIR

NANA-AMA DANQUAH

W. W. NORTON & COMPANY

Celebrating a Century of Independent Publishing

Foreword copyright © 2023 by Andrew Solomon, reprinted by permission of The Wylie Agency LLC

Copyright © 2023, 1998 by Meri Nana-Ama Danquah

All rights reserved
Printed in the United States of America
Reissued as a Norton paperback 2023

Since this page cannot legally accomodate all the copyright notices, pages 299–300 consitute an extension of the copyright page.

For information about permission to reproduce selections from this book, write to Permissions, W. W. Norton & Company, Inc., 500 Fifth Avenue, New York, NY 10110

Desktop composition by Platinum Manuscript Services
Manufacturing by Lakeside Book Company
Book design by Guenet Abraham

Library of Congress Cataloging-in-Publication Data

Danquah, Meri Nana-Ama.
Willow weep for me : a black woman's journey through depression : a memoir / by Meri Nana-Ama Danquah.
p.   cm.
ISBN 0-393-04567-6
1. Danquah, Meri Nana-Ama—Mental Health. 2. Depressed persons—United States—Biography. 3. Afro-American women—Biography. I. Title.
RC537.D295 1998
616.85'27'0092—dc21
[b] 97-20515
CIP

ISBN 978-1-324-05061-2 pbk.

W. W. Norton & Company, Inc., 500 Fifth Avenue, New York, NY 10110
http://www.wwnorton.com

W. W. Norton & Company Ltd., 35 Carlisle Street, London W1D 3BS

1 2 3 4 5 6 7 8 9 0

To

David Godoy-Hatcher
Always, this friendship . . .

Paula Danquah-Brobby
Through distance and silence, still . . .

Andrew W. Solomon
The laughter, the love, the loyalty; as faithful and true as a book, you are . . .

the late Gregory Stephen Tate
Our river flows on, my friend; our conversation continues; there will be no end . . .

———————◆———————

FOR

Korama A. Danquah
My everything.

Acknowledgments

———◆———

THE WAY *WILLOW WEEP FOR ME* came into the world twenty-five years ago proved to me that there are things we are called to do, each and every one of us.

Thank you to my then editor at the *Washington Post*, Jefferson Morley, for commissioning an article after a random but passionate conversation about depression, and then seeing a book in the mess of pages I later sent him.

Fate then landed those pages in the capable and nurturing hands of my former literary agent, Anne Edelstein, and my editor, Jill Bialosky, both of whom took a personal interest in the book and understood the importance and urgency of mental health awareness. I will forever be grateful to them.

I would like to also acknowledge and sing the praises of

my friend, Cindy Spiegel, for reading and giving invaluable editorial advice on the original manuscript.

My literary agent, Tanya McKinnon, is one of the most brilliant, insightful, and visionary human beings I have ever met. This reissue of the memoir exists because of Tanya's unwavering support of me and belief in my work—and I am deeply grateful to her for both.

I feel much gratitude, as well, for the friendship and generosity of Emily Bernard, a gifted writer and dedicated literary citizen. It was through her insistence and connection that Tanya and I started working together.

Many thanks to the Djerassi Resident Artists Program for providing space and solitude. Considerable portions of *Willow Weep for Me* were written during my 1995 residency. I am thankful to the Artists Community Federal Credit Union, the PEN America Writers Emergency Fund, and the Carnegie Fund for Authors for their financial assistance during the initial writing of this book, without which I would have had to set aside this project. I feel so blessed to have been able to work with the patient and compassionate Drew Elizabeth Weitman to meet all the deadlines and other administrative requirements for this edition of the book.

Throughout my life, regardless of whatever difficulties, I have always been blessed with many wonderful friendships. Unfortunately, I'm unable to list everyone who has helped, supported, and loved me through the ups and downs over the years. Even if your name is not here, please know that I hold you in my heart, and that I am grateful for your presence in and contributions to my life. Thank you to the *real* Jade Parsons, Scott Riley, Patricia Bledsoe, and Eugene

ACKNOWLEDGMENTS

Bledsoe. Thanks, also, to Eric Burns, Nola Kambanda, George Kelly, Jackson Browne, Natina Hopson, Dan Simon, Frank Roman, Anne Sackey, Ray Santos & Michael Mann, Tonita Austin, David Vigliano, Emma Sweeney, Michael Gottfried, Bill Campbell, Gideon Rosman, Shea Gipson, Susanna Bech-Young, Nana Addo Dankwa Akufo-Addo, Cessily Walker, John Dramani Mahama, Steven Biller, Vanessa Estelle Williams, Eriq LaSalle, Ernest Kwame Nkrumah Addo, Nnamdi Mowetta, Hill Harper, Annie Burrows, W. Steven Temple, Bridgid Coulter, Joseph Stern, Lily Buor, Jaime Pressly, George Patriot Seymore, Amir Soltani, and my brilliant cousin, Kwasi Twum.

All praises to my sister circle, the women who hold space and carry the highest vision of me, even when I am unable to myself: Stephanie Covington Armstrong, Lisa Jones Brown, Ama Dadson, Stephanie Han, CCH Pounder, Bee-be Smith, Karen Grose, Anedra Shockley, Tchise Ajé, Michelle Herndon, Pamela Starks, Anna Bossman, Kimball Stroud, Uduak Amimo, Jennifer Pastiloff, Lisa Pegram, Kate Connor, Phaedra Parks, Ipeleng Kgositsile, and my incredible cousin, Nana Ofori-Atta Tatiboit.

For my friends, fellow wordsmiths who inspire and challenge me on the page and in our conversations and correspondence, I stand up in awe and celebration. Thank you: Mzee Ngugi wa Thiong'o, Jeffery Renard Allen, Toni Ann Johnson, Susan Hayden, Kwame Dawes, Laura Stanfill, David Goldsmith, Lidia Yuknavitch, Cheryl Strayed, Jonetta Rose Barras, Bassey Ikpi, Samantha Dunn, Gail Wronsky, Shay Youngblood, Danzy Senna, Patrick Smith, Vanessa Mártir, Doug Adrianson, Nina Sankovitch, Nadia

Owusu, Cynthia Bond, Chimamanda Ngozi Adichie, Joe Donnelly, Imbolo Mbue, Nastashia Minto, Lisa Teasley, Elissa Altman, Cassandra Lane, Jane Ratcliffe, Elizabeth Earley, Whitney Otto, and Monika Drake, and my multi-talented cousin, Nana Oforiatta Ayim.

After *Willow Weep for Me* was first published, some family members called me crazy, a liar. I was prepared for that hostility, the attempt to discredit me and my experiences because I challenged the accepted narratives and sanitized images that were being presented to the public. This sort of reprisal is why so many people stay silent in their pain, refusing to speak their truth. What I was not prepared for was my father reading the book and then saying to me, "I know you told the truth. I believe you. And I am sorry for all the hurt and pain that my absence allowed to come into your life." Do you know what it means for a survivor of abuse, any type of abuse, to speak their truth and be told, "I believe you"? My father, N. Duke Brobby, with whom I'd had a strained, often acrimonious, sometimes volatile relationship, chose healing over ego, fear, and shame. Daddy, your words that day—so powerful and filled with compassion for us both—continue to be a balm. I love you.

When I am at my weakest, I summon strength from my ancestor-and-angel squad. I thank them for watching over and protecting me: Dr. JB Danquah, Comfort Vesta Carboo, Gifty Carboo, Paul Walcott-Danquah, Maya Angelou, Jeff Young, Anne Beatts, Kofi Awoonor, Ama Ata Aidoo, James Bernard Hawkins, Don Mensah, Kofi Blankson Ocansey, Florence Tate, Gregory Stephen Tate, and my beloved cousins, JB Danquah-Adu and Ferdinand Ayim.

ACKNOWLEDGMENTS

Finally, I want to thank the young(er) people in my life, who give me tremendous hope for a tomorrow that is defined by equality, wellness, peace, and art: my bonus sons Christopher Logan, José-Samuel Clair, and Shafik Mahama; my bonus daughter Angie Hilem; Shane Browne, Chantel Whittle, Mike Makowsky, Kat Boorstein, Cathleen Cher Chen, Emily Sears, Clarissa Bannor, Anniwaa Buachie, my best foodie friend Harper Wayne and, again and again forever, my darling daughter, Korama A. Danquah.

FOREWORD

On Weeping

———————

ANDREW SOLOMON

I MET NANA-AMA DANQUAH at a depression conference in St. Louis when we were both on the circuit of speakers discussing mental illness. It was an unlikely hatching ground for a life's friendship, but among that dreary crowd of suicidologists, Nana-Ama stood out for her trademark mix of deep thinking, compassion, and fabulous style, and I immediately wanted to know her better. That was twenty-five years ago, when we were both greener. We promptly read each other's work. Although depression in general was scantily acknowledged at that point, depression among people of color was a topic almost entirely untouched, and depression among Black women was forbidden territory. You could find characters who sounded depressed in Toni Morrison's or Gloria Naylor's fictions, and you could hear the anguish in Billie Holiday's voice, but there was no previous memoir that dwelt on the topic as *Willow Weep for Me* did. This remains a brave book in our more confessional decade, but at the time of its writing, it was humblingly audacious.

The intersection of mental health and identity politics is not well explored. Depression is depression is depression; the symptoms are essentially the same for everyone. But both the origins of and the solutions to those problems vary from one community to the next. As a gay white man, I had very few models when I was first clinically depressed; Nana-Ama had none. We know that depression shows very little regard for race or income or any other demographic determinant. Often, however, it exists in tandem with trauma, and trauma runs high among Black Americans in a racist society. Depression sets in when someone with a biological vulnerability has that vulnerability triggered by external circumstances. If the original vulnerability is very strong, the triggers can be slight; if the vulnerability is less pronounced, then the triggers have to be stronger.

Black women, as Nana-Ama points out, inhabit a culture that expects them to wrestle with their own minds without bothering anyone else, and to be strong above all. Some Black Americans use the trope of having survived slavery as an indication that they should be able to survive anything. An African immigrant, Nana-Ama is descended from statesmen rather than from enslaved people, but growing up largely in the United States, she absorbed Black American cultural norms and they combined with elements of pride and social confidence endemic to her Ghanaian heritage to leave her intolerant of frailty in others or in herself. She had to battle her own personality to triumph over one of its core characteristics.

It seems ironic that so much of the Black community is uneasy with the language of mental illness even though the triggers for Black people in America today are often so acute. Nana-Ama describes long cycles of neglect and abuse: from her absent father, her overbearing-yet-withdrawn mother, her mother's sexually exploitative boyfriend. Her book addresses, in startling and awful detail, the pain of a precocious sexuality that led to repeated violations of her trust. It recounts episodes of outright racism, both in the context of her poverty and during her ventures into the upper echelons of privilege. Her descriptions of cruelty, subtle and explicit, tear a reader's heart. Sometimes, her will to survive seems Sisyphean; whatever was demanded of her is followed by harder demands, and harder ones yet.

Willow chronicles the terrible strains of life as a single mother. It reckons with poverty and limns a complex relationship between financial and emotional desolation. It recounts saving a friend from suicide. It deals with how understanding other people's depression can liberate even as it engenders empathetic distress. Its underlying topic is the aloneness that is endemic to all depression, but that is particularly afflictive for Black women, who have not only the disapproving callousness of the culture at large but also, often, an indomitable force of denial among their intimates. Instead of sympathy, there are exhortations to prayer. Instead of compassion, there is a culture in which "holding it together" is the ultimate mark of integrity— even of womanhood. You bear children and you bear your anguish. Woven through this book is Nana-Ama's courageous decision to shatter that imperative to secrecy and its consequent silence. In breaking that silence, she discovered legions of Black women (and others) who were struggling with depression. She discovered that experiences she had deemed humiliatingly private were, in fact, commonplace.

Motherhood seems to have been both the fact that saved Nana-Ama and the burden that overwhelmed her. She did not have the luxury of ceasing to function. Against steep odds, she managed to raise a daughter who is already beautiful and talented in these pages, but who has gone on to become an authentic success in nearly every aspect of life and who remains profoundly attached to Nana-Ama. Producing children who are happy and who in adulthood still want to spend time with you is perhaps life's toughest job, an ideal that can be grossly undermined when a mother battles mental illness. In these pages, Nana-Ama worries about her depressions damaging her relationship to her daughter and describes the heroic lengths she went to in her determination that it do no such thing. She recognizes the depressive element in her own mother, too, and achieves forgiveness after a long history of stress and resentment.

Nana-Ama ultimately describes what it is like to experience depression without the nomenclature to communicate your symptoms, much less the technologies, interventions, and philosophical constructs to overcome them. Pain radiates off every page here, a frightening pain around which loom terrible consequences; seldom has anyone given a more affecting portrait of how it feels to be just barely holding on with a very dubious safety net. Nana-Ama chronicles the difficult work of accepting her own mind's fragility. For Nana-

Ama, acknowledging her depression meant inventing a new identity, one that held not only her race, her womanhood, her experience as an immigrant, her financial struggles, and her personal history, but also her mental health. Integrating a new identity with an existing identity is a lifetime's work. Nana-Ama's prose is unusually lucid in describing how she had to reinvent herself in the wake of severe depression—and how she had to reimagine the world around her.

I was touched but surprised when Nana-Ama asked me to write this foreword—touched because I love the book and love her, but surprised because I am neither Black nor a woman. But sometimes love matters as much as identity. Nana-Ama and I have seen each other through rough times; we have tolerated each other's moments of shaky mental health. I have witnessed her force-of-nature determination, the endurance she learned in part by writing this book.

Willow Weep for Me is testament to Nana-Ama's wish to turn her anguish into something that can help others. It is explicit about her worst experiences, but devoid of self-pity. It can be harrowing to read, but its openness is also an authentic comfort. Her vulnerability has made her more responsive to other people's vulnerability, and her book bends toward kindness. It is more salient now than it was when it was first published, as the country returns to overt racism; as police brutality is recorded daily; as half of the country remains unwilling to discuss, let alone address, systemic racism; as racial bias in health care plays out in the pandemic. Child suicide is up among Black youth more than in any other ethnic group. The crisis has arrived.

As her friend, I know that Nana-Ama has a gift for celebration; she sometimes posts videos of herself dancing on her own in front of her bookshelf at home, and they make me want to join the party, even when I know she is merely cheering herself up. Her book, like the dancing, is a mechanism of healing for both herself and those who encounter her. The willow may weep for Nana-Ama Danquah, but I cheer for her. This introduction is only a sliver of my applause.

ANDREW SOLOMON
New York
February 2023

Look not upon me, because I am black,

because the sun hath looked upon me:

my mother's children were angry with me;

they made me the keeper of the vineyards;

but mine own vineyard have I not kept.

—Song of Solomon 1:6–7

WILLOW WEEP *for* ME

THERE ARE ALWAYS fresh flowers and plants in my house. When they begin to die it is a sure sign that I, too, am beginning to wither. The window shades are never closed. Sunshine must always be visible. The bedroom is littered with no less than four alarm clocks. None display the same time. Some are as little as fifteen minutes ahead, others as much as one hour. Each night I set the clocks for a wake-up time of 6:00 AM. Rarely am I out of bed before 7:30 AM. Mornings have always been difficult.

For most of my life I have nurtured a consistent, low-grade melancholy; I have been addicted to despair. Because of my habitual tardiness, an eighth-grade teacher once scrawled these words of advice in my yearbook: *Once you learn to wake up in the morning, life will be a breeze.*

Though I have attended college in many places and at many times, I do not yet hold a degree. I have worked as a word processor, secretary, file clerk, waitress, arts administrator, phone sex operator, and creative writing instructor. I am often working-class broke. I am also a single mother. Life, for me, has hardly been "a breeze."

The majority of my days begin like this:

Barely awake, I head for the bathroom, stare into the mirror until I can identify the person staring back. There are still those mornings when my image seems foreign to me, when I move through my house like an intruder, fumbling over furniture and walking into walls, trying to avoid the temptation to crouch inside a corner and just zone out. "It gets better." I promise myself as I make my way into the living room, "This day *will* get better. It has to."

Having sworn off most chemical mood-altering substances, I choose music over coffee and cigarettes. Music eases my depressed mood. I have come to rely on one song as my morning prayer. I sit and listen to the words, allow them to reach out, like hands, and lift me to a more sacred state of consciousness. They affirm life as something worth living despite this pain I sometimes carry.

> I want to live in the world, not inside my head
> I want to live in the world, I want to stand and be counted

Music and motion are the two things that can immediately touch the hurt inside of me. I can't begin to count the number of times I have circled Los Angeles in my car, traveling from one freeway onto the next without any particular destination, the tape player blasting tunes, my mouth open wide enough to scream lyrics.

There was a time when at any given moment I would abandon my bed, my lover, my apartment, to literally drive away the depression. The slow, gentle rhythm of automobiles, trains, and buses surrounds and soothes me, like an infant that is being cradled into calmness. But being a mother has changed the ways in which I mother myself. No matter how deep the despair or urgent the need to flee, I can't abandon my daughter. Nor can I drape her sleeping body in thick blankets, toss her over my shoulder like some runaway's sack and take her with me. She relies on my presence, my ability to cope.

Emotionally and physically taxing, the responsibilities of parenting are overwhelming for even the most stable people. Imagine them for someone with a history of depression stretching as far as a late-afternoon shadow. The daily tasks—bathing, ironing clothes, dressing, braiding hair, making breakfast, preparing lunch, school drop-offs and pick-ups—require every bit of what little get-up-and-go I have. However, they define my day. These responsibilities help me move past the temptation to rationalize myself right back into bed. Most times.

Afternoons and early evenings are usually my best and most productive times, when I am able to concentrate and focus without fatigue or anxiety. Sleep plays a major role in my efforts to maintain a balanced mood. I have found that too much is as disruptive as not enough. Late evenings, like mornings, take a harsh toll. I vacillate from insomnia to hypersomnia, from not being able to get a wink of rest to oversleeping and constantly feeling drugged with exhaustion.

We have all, to some degree, experienced days of depression. Days when nothing is going our way, when even the most trivial events can trigger tears, when all we want to do is crawl into a hole and ask "Why me?" For most people, these are isolated occurrences. When the day ends, so too does the sadness. But for some, such as myself, the depression doesn't lift at the end of the day or disappear when others try to cheer us up. These feelings of helplessness and desperation worsen and grow into a full-blown clinical depression. And when depression reaches clinical proportions, it *is* truly an illness, not a character flaw or an insignificant bout with the blues that an individual can "snap out of" at will.

Our reality often comes to us in fragments. From 1989 to 1994, I experienced several episodes of major depression. I prolonged the pain with silence, mostly because I was afraid—of being misunderstood or ostracized, of losing friends, of losing respect. Unless it has touched your life, depression can be a difficult disease to understand. I certainly would have never thought to consider myself a depressive. Clinical depression simply did not exist within the realm of my possibilities; or, for that matter, within the realm of possibilities for any of the black women in my world.

The illusion of strength has been and continues to be of

major significance to me as a black woman. The one myth that I have had to endure my entire life is that of my supposed birthright to strength. Black women are *supposed* to be strong—caretakers, nurturers, healers of other people—any of the twelve dozen variations of Mammy. Emotional hardship is *supposed* to be built into the structure of our lives. It went along with the territory of being both black and female in a society that completely undervalues the lives of black people and regards all women as second-class citizens. It seemed that suffering, for a black woman, was part of the package.

Or so I thought.

Not so long ago, a friend invited me to a dinner party. I was standing with a small group of people deeply immersed in conversation. I was the only person of color in the group. My thoughts drifted from the conversation. To pull me back into the discussion, my friend asked about my writing. An older, heavily perfumed woman standing with us wanted to know what I was writing.

"A book about black women and depression," my friend volunteered.

"*Black* women and depression?" the woman threw out sarcastically. "Isn't that kinda redundant?" The people standing around us exchanged abrasive chuckles.

"Don't get me wrong," the woman continued, taking a sip of her cocktail. There wasn't a hint of apology in her voice. "It's just that when *black* women start going on Prozac, you know the whole world is falling apart." I was instantly filled with outrage, anger, and hurt.

"When black women start going on Prozac, *their* whole world has already fallen apart. They're just trying to piece it back together," I said. Months later, I am still unable to shake the echo of that woman's comments. I have replayed the scene a thousand times in my mind, each time giving what I felt was a more fitting, stinging reply. Ironically, I do understand the reasons for her comment.

Stereotypes and clichés about mental illness are as pervasive as those about race. I have noticed that the mental illness that affects white men is often characterized, if not glamorized, as a sign of genius, a burden of cerebral superiority, artistic eccentricity—as if their depression is somehow heroic. White women who suffer from mental illness are depicted as idle, spoiled, or just plain hysterical. Black men are demonized and pathologized. Black women with psychological problems are certainly not seen as geniuses; we are generally not labeled "hysterical" or "eccentric" or even "pathological." When a black woman suffers from a mental disorder, the overwhelming opinion is that she is weak. And weakness in black women is intolerable.

There is a poem by E. Ethelbert Miller that always comes to mind when I think of how hard it sometimes is for black women to be seen as vulnerable and emotionally complex. It is simply titled "Billie Holiday":

sometimes the deaf
hear better than the blind

some men
when they first
heard her sing

were only attracted
to the flower in her hair

Sadly, it is not only white people who are unable to see beyond the ornamentation that is placed on black women's lives. I have had conversations about my depression with black people—both men and women—that were similar to the one I had with the white woman at the dinner party. I've frequently been told things like: "Girl, you've been hanging out with too many white folk"; "What do you have to be depressed about? If our people could make it through slavery, we can make it through anything"; "Take your troubles to Jesus, not no damn psychiatrist."

When there aren't dismissive questions, patronizing statements, or ludicrous suggestions, there is silence. As if there are no acceptable ways, no appropriate words to begin a dialogue about this illness. And, given the oppressive nature of the existing language surrounding depression, perhaps for black people there really aren't any.

You've heard descriptions of depression before: A black hole; an enveloping darkness; a dismal existence through which no light shines; the black dog; darkness, and more darkness. But what does darkness mean to me, a woman who has spent her life surrounded by it? The darkness of my skin; the darkness of my friends and family. I have never been afraid of the dark. It poses no harm to me. What is the color of my depression?

Depression offers layers, textures, noises. At times depression is as flimsy as a feather, barely penetrating the surface of my life, hovering like a slight halo of pessimism. Other times it comes on gradually like a common cold or a storm, each day presenting new signals and symptoms until finally I am drowning in it. Most times, in its most superficial and seductive sense, it is rich and enticing. A field of velvet waiting to embrace me. It is loud and dizzying, inviting the tenors and screeching sopranos of thoughts, unrelenting sadness, and the sense of impending doom. Depression is all of these things to me—but darkness, it is not.

———◆———

won't you celebrate with me

what I have shaped into

a kind of life? i had no model.

born in babylon

both nonwhite and woman

what did i see to be except myself?

i made it up

here on this bridge between

starshine and clay,

my one hand holding tight

my other hand; come celebrate

with me that everyday

something has tried to kill me

and has failed.

—Lucille Clifton

BETWEEN STARSHINE
and CLAY

———◆———

MY RELATIONSHIP WITH depression began long before I noticed it. The first conscious thought that all was not well with me came in 1989, when I was twenty-two. I had been living in Los Angeles for two years, working various temp jobs while trying to establish myself as a writer and performance artist. Out of nowhere and for no apparent reason— or so it seemed—I started feeling strong sensations of grief. I don't remember the step-by-step progression of the illness. What I can recall is that my life disintegrated; first, into a strange and terrifying space of sadness and then, into a cobweb of fatigue. I gradually lost my ability to function. It would take me hours to get up out of bed, get bathed, put clothes on. By the time I was fully dressed, it was well into the afternoon.

When I went out into the city, I would always become disoriented, often spacing out behind the wheel of my car or in the middle of a sentence. My thoughts would just disappear. I'd forget where I was driving to, the point I was about to make in conversation. It was as if my synapses were misfiring, my brain off kilter. A simple stroll to the coffee shop down the block overloaded my senses: sounds of feet shuffling on sidewalks, honks from cars, blinking of traffic lights, loud colors of clothing. It was all bewildering. I started to have panic attacks every time I went outside.

After a while I stopped showing up at my temp job, stopped going out altogether, and locked myself in my home. It was over three weeks before I felt well enough to leave. During that time, I cut myself off from everything and everyone. Days would go by before I bathed. I did not have enough energy to clean up myself or my home. There was a trail of undergarments and other articles of clothing that ran from the living room to the bedroom to the bathroom of my tiny apartment. Dishes with decaying food covered every counter and tabletop in the place. Even watching TV or talking on the phone required too much concentration. All I could do was take to my pallet of blankets and coats positioned on the living room floor and wait for whatever I was going through to pass.

And it did. Slowly. That's the thing about depression, it will generally vanish on its own. The problem is that there is no telling when it will go away or for how long it will stay gone. When I felt better I bathed, took the garbage out, did laundry, plugged my telephone back in, and made plans to venture forth into the weird outside.

The first person to call me was an actress friend who wanted to brag about her trip to Berlin. She proudly told me that she had recently returned with a piece of the Wall. "The Berlin Wall?" I asked in disbelief. The last time I had heard mention of the Berlin Wall was in a high-school history class. My friend had to start from square one and explain to me that the Berlin Wall had come down.

"Wait, wait, wait. Like, you don't know? You're joking, right? My gosh, Meri, where've you been, Mars?"

It was humiliating. I felt like Rip Van Winkle. During the time I was laid up in my apartment making huge efforts to do simple things like brush my teeth and pull open the curtains, people had traveled, landscapes had changed; the world as I had known it before I surrendered and crawled into bed was no more. There was no escaping that episode without acknowledging that something extraordinary had happened to me. Ordinary folks just don't hole themselves up for weeks on end without bathing, working, reading the newspaper, talking to friends, or watching TV. Deep down, I knew that something had gone wrong with me, in me. But what could I do?

Stunned and defenseless, the only thing I felt I could do was move on. I assured myself that my mind and the behaviors it provoked were well within my control. In the future I would just have to be extremely aware. I would make sure that what happened did not happen again. But it did. Again and again, no matter how aware, responsible, or in control I tried to be. Each time, I buried the fear. I chastised myself for not paying attention to my emotions, for allowing myself to sink to such disgusting depths.

Each wave of the depression cost me something dear. I lost my job because the temp agencies where I was registered could no longer tolerate my lengthy absences. Unable to pay rent, I lost my apartment and ended up having to rent a small room in a boarding house. I lost my friends. Most of them found it too troublesome to deal with my sudden moodiness and passivity so they stopped calling and coming around. There were some that tried to hang in there and be supportive, but before long the depression took its toll on those relationships as well. Whenever I resurfaced from my episodes of depression, it was too hard to pick up where we had left off. "You've changed," my friends told me. "You're not the same person." How could I be? How could anyone be the same after their entire world has come to a screeching halt?

Thankfully, there were a few major reprieves, weeks, sometimes months, when it seemed as if the nails of despair weren't digging as deeply into my skin. During one of these times, I entered a new relationship.

———◆———

IN EARLY 1990, I met Justin Armah, a tall, bespectacled thirty-eight-year-old accountant from Ghana, my native country. He was, on the surface, everything I believed I wanted a mate to be: charming, ambitious, and employed. We met at "Positive Vibrations Through Spoken Word," a twice-monthly poetry series, which I founded and organized at Rosalind's, a small Ethiopian restaurant in Los Angeles. He learned about the readings through *LA Weekly*, an alternative newspaper, which had recently featured me in its "Local Heroes" segment. As an active participant in the literary community, I was just beginning to gain a bit of recognition for my work as a writer and events organizer.

Justin and I quickly became romantically involved. We suffocated each other with our constant togetherness. After a few weeks, I moved into his home, a two-bedroom duplex on the west side of town. It was the perfect solution come right on time. What I felt I needed in my life was an anchor in case I began to drift away again. I hoped my relationship with Justin would be that grounding force. Depression is a very "*me*" disease. There is an enormous amount of self-criticism, self-loathing, and low self-esteem. Everything revolves around the perception of self. Most depressives find themselves—as much to their own disgust as to everybody else's—annoyingly and negatively self-obsessed.

I was not so much in love with Justin as I was with the prospect of having someone other than myself be the focal point of my life. We were not at all a compatible pair. There was a sixteen-year age difference between us. He was a stable, well-established professional. I was the opposite—a college drop-out who spent the bulk of her time writing poetry, something he eventually began to ridicule as a futile, unproductive hobby. Whatever forces of passion, lust, or need that brought us together disappeared as quickly as they appeared. By that time, I was already pregnant.

The pregnancy was an added point of contention between us. Justin wanted me to abort. Motherhood was not something to which I had ever aspired but for some reason I could not bring myself to end the pregnancy. There was another life inside of me, growing, changing my physical form, and I loved it. But morning sickness and the stress of a failing relationship turned what should have been a joyous time into a thick, lengthy period of depression. I grew increasingly unhappy and agitated. Very little brought me pleasure. Everything seemed complicated and burdensome, including "Positive Vibrations Through Spoken Word," my reading series. Eventually I stopped organizing it. I even stopped writing. It seemed as if the world was closing in on me, squeezing me dry.

There was no one close by that I felt I could rely on or confide in. My parents, though divorced, both lived in Washington, D.C. Ordinarily, we were not very close, but throughout the course of my pregnancy I spoke with them pretty frequently. At the time, my relationship with them could be described, at best, as turbulent. However, being able to talk to them, no matter how short or shallow the conversations, made me feel like I was not alone, like someone cared.

In my seventh month of pregnancy, my mother and father flew to L.A. to attend my baby shower and to meet Justin. It was a tremendous display of love for them, to take leave from their lives, at my request, to share the occasion with me. Still, I found their visit to be particularly traumatizing. When they arrived, all the underlying issues that had inspired me to move and place the distance of an entire country between us came with them. Suddenly, I felt like a child, not a woman carrying a child.

Like my parents, Justin had immigrated to the States as an adult, so the three of them carried on for hours about schools they had attended and friends they had in common. I had nothing to offer the discussion. I was either too young or too estranged from Ghanaian culture. They even talked to each other in *Twi*, a language I can't speak and have trouble understanding. I felt shut out. The remarks that were meant for me to hear were made in English. These remarks were generally jokes made by my mother about my inability to cook or clean house properly and my flair for melodrama—all faults I had supposedly acquired because I was too Americanized.

It was a pretty devastating experience to have my parents come and belittle me in front of a man who belittled me on a daily basis. To say the least, it wreaked havoc on my self-esteem. At one point during the visit, Justin took us out to dinner at an elegant Chinese restaurant in Beverly Hills. During our meal, my mother made a remark that upset me. I don't remember what it was. So many things that my parents said and did during that trip were upsetting but, for the most part, I never let them know that. To do so in Justin's presence would have caused them embarrassment.

From the age of six, I was raised in the United States. Like many other immigrant children, I grew up trying to find my own personal balance between two distinct cultures. I have always felt torn between the rigid mores of Ghanaian culture and the overly permissive attitudes of Americans. If a choice had to be made that evening, I felt obligated to err on the side of heritage. By remaining stoic and non-responsive, I hoped to disprove my parents' accusations that I had become too Americanized. Before I could stop myself though, I started sobbing hysterically over my meal. Mum, Dad, and Justin were dumbfounded. They looked at each other curiously. I excused myself from the table, rushed through the dimly lit restaurant and headed for the bathroom, knowing that I had only proved them right. I was melodramatic, thin-skinned, and whiny, just like their image of the average American.

When I returned, Mum and Justin made jest of my outburst. My father seemed genuinely concerned.

"Are you sure you're alright?" he asked, gently placing his hand on my back. His concern came a little too late.

"Yeah, Daddy. I'll be fine," I said coolly, pulling my chair closer to the table. For the rest of the evening and, the rest of their visit, I wore an armor of indifference.

In hindsight, I must admit that I was being oversensitive. My emotions were delicate enough that any comment, however innocent, could have easily been perceived as negative and prompted tears. Nevertheless, that evening was as accurate a representation as any of the way my parents and I related to each other. They criticized, I cried. We were complete strangers to one another. Like many children of divorce, I felt abandoned by them at a time in my childhood when I needed them most, and the disappointment of that stayed with me in my young adulthood.

Becoming a parent has enabled me to see my own parents as fragile and fallible people. Understanding how difficult it is to raise a child in the face of life's unpredictable circumstances, I no longer find myself standing in such harsh judgment of them or the choices that they made so long ago. I believe that my individual therapy was instrumental in bringing me to this point.

When I first started therapy, I found myself unable to talk about my parents or admit that I felt a tremendous amount of rage toward them. I imagine that it was because in African as well as African-American cultures, talking about one's parents is frowned upon; only an ingrate would do such a thing. Even talking about other people's parents is a no-no. When I was a kid, the worst thing you could say to somebody was "Yo' Mama." That was like an invitation to a fight.

I have often heard it said that depression is anger turned inward. I don't know how true this is, but there is no denying that the events of my childhood played a major role in fostering my vulnerability to depression. In fact, it is believed that an individual's susceptibility to depressive disorders is usually formed early in childhood, especially with people who have experienced traumatic loss. This theory notwithstanding, I doubt that the unspoken anger that has fueled my depressions was caused solely by my parents. Suffice it to say, the pain that has already passed between us could claim a lifetime of tears.

———◆———

EARLIER IN MY PREGNANCY, I had taken a full-time administrative assistant position in a one-person office. My boss was rarely there so I spent my days alone. In the evenings, Justin and I kept our distance. We rarely talked, and when we did it was only to argue. I became completely withdrawn. There was a great deal of time on my hands and I used it to think. For hours, I sat and thought. And thought. I thought about my life, how hard I was trying to hold on to it, how fast it was sliding out of my hands. Many times I thought about ending it.

Whenever I went to my prenatal appointments, I shared my feelings of depression with Dr. Woods, my obstetrician. "Aaah, those hormones," he would say. I still find it surprising that he never suggested I see a psychiatrist or get into some other form of counseling. The intake forms I filled out before my first appointment had a list of ailments and conditions that, based upon medical history and family background, patients were supposed to check *yes* or *no* to. I specifically remember checking *yes* next to *Depression* and then being instructed to list medications and/or hospitalizations.

Having, at that time, never been medicated or hospitalized for depression, I went back and scratched out my *yes* and placed a checkmark in the *no* column. One would think that either Dr. Woods or the nurses reviewing those forms would have asked me why I had checked *yes* to begin with. Sure, it could have been a mistake, a slip of the wrist, but a simple question might have revealed a couple of tell-tale symptoms, raised a few eyebrows. Maybe it could have even given us some insight as to why I eventually developed pre-eclampsia (also known as toxemia), a pregnancy-related illness usually brought on by stress or hypertension.

The progression of pre-eclampsia can be monitored and somewhat retarded through rest, alterations in diet, and regular prenatal care but the illness can only be halted by the termination of one's pregnancy. As a result of the pre-eclampsia, my blood pressure soared to a deadly high. Through artificial induction of labor, my pregnancy was terminated in the ninth month, a few days before my due date. For nearly thirty hours I lay suspended in an excruciating purgatory. When the doctors told me that I was, at long last, fully dilated and that they could see the baby's head, I prepared to push.

With my eyes closed all that was visible to me was darkness. I imagined it to be the same darkness surrounding the baby in my womb. A nurturing and protective sky without stars, without clouds. A blank space of all that was possible. An eternity waiting to be defined. For the first time in months, perhaps years, I felt safe and complete, in that darkness. If death was this peaceful then I wanted it. If life could be so full of the power and potential I felt right then, I craved it as well.

After my daughter, Korama Afua, was born I was allowed to hold her for a few minutes before the doctors shifted me onto another gurney and rushed me into the Maternity ICU.

CAUSES OF POSTPARTUM DEPRESSION (PPD)

Factors that are believed to contribute to PPD include the following: genetic predisposition (i.e., presence of depression in a blood relative); chronic sleep deprivation and fatigue; colicky, hard-to-care-for babies; dramatic hormonal changes; medical complications in either mother or infant; a predisposition to self-criticism; previous postpartum or other type of clinical depression; absence of support from family or friends; and/or isolation.*

At home, Justin and I resumed our acrimonious partnership. Our arguments began to get physical. We rarely saw one another because he started staying at the office until late in the evenings. I was perpetually tired. Luckily, Korama was a low-maintenance infant. She rarely cried except when she needed to be nursed or diapered and she slept soundly for long stretches of time. Mostly, she would just lie there next to me in bed and stare. Her look haunted me. I felt as if she sensed my ineptitude, knew in her tiny heart that she

*This Isn't What I Expected: Recognizing and Recovering from Depression and Anxiety After Childbirth, by Karen R. Kleiman, M.S.W., and Valerie D. Raskin, M.D. New York: Bantam, 1994.

had been shortchanged by the heavens and granted a mother that was no more capable of dealing with the world than she.

These were dangerous times. The feelings of power and potential I felt during her birth dissolved into fear. I was afraid all the time. Afraid of all that existed beyond my front door, afraid of all that existed within. Love can often inspire people to persevere, especially the love of a child. Surely Justin and I could work it out, if we both tried. I convinced myself of this each night as I watched the clock, waiting for him to come home. I just wanted so badly for it to work, for everything to fall into place. But Justin had never loved me. I knew this. My needs had never been his wants. A baby changed nothing. He stayed away as much as he could. In June of 1991, two months after Korama was born, Justin threw us out.

Korama and I moved into an apartment in a run-down building that I agreed to manage in exchange for free rent. I taught creative writing part-time, and more nights than I care to remember were spent working a phone sex line out of my home. A dense cloud of melancholy hung over my head. This time around the depression did not display itself as it had before. Instead of being overtired, sleepy, mournful, and confused, I had insomnia and developed obsessive-compulsive tendencies.

Cleanliness and organization became my constant pre-occupation. The closets had to be arranged so that the shoes were lined up from small to large and the clothes were hung by color and length—light to dark, short to long. Books had to be shelved alphabetically. Korama and I had to be washed, pressed, dressed, and neat, at all times. This tendency to create order exists in my nondepressed personality as well. Depression merely pushes it to the extreme. I have always been very pragmatic and detail-oriented. If I can't maintain control over the conditions and relationships in my life, I control my household and the things within it because it eases my anxiety.

The one thing I was desperately trying to get a handle on was the situation with Justin, which had become completely out of control. He offered no financial assistance. His only contribution to our survival was his presence, in all its uselessness and unpredictability. We had no formal visitation schedule, but he stopped by sporadically to visit his daughter. When he came over—usually without advance notice— he would merely stand over Korama's bassinet smiling and cooing, waving his long, dark fingers in front of her face as if to say hello. Rarely would he change a diaper or give a feeding.

My heart was like a cauldron of poisonous emotions. I despised Justin for what he had done to me. I vowed to never again give anyone the opportunity to hurt me. Yet I allowed him constant access to both me and Korama and eventually I began sleeping with him again. You see, it was not him that I truly despised. It was me. I hated myself for not being chosen. For not being whatever it was that he and everybody else wanted me to be. By sleeping with him, I thought I could somehow bring myself closer to being the woman I had been unable to be. A woman worthy of love or, at the very least, of respect and humane treatment. It was illogical and twisted, I know, but so are most conclusions drawn in a depressed state of mind—for instance, my initial conclusion that Justin was the sort of individual I would want as a mate.

From the beginning, our relationship was a formula for disaster. Depressed people often attract unhealthy relationships and inadvertently subject themselves, and their already battered self-image, to additional abuse. It is like a self-fulfilling prophecy. You feel as if you are worthless so you attach yourself to someone who you think will give your life some meaning, be a safe harbor for your soul. But only you can protect what's inside.

I finally realized this when, for the last time, our relationship escalated to physical violence. One evening when Justin stopped by, presumably to visit his daughter, we got into an argument. I asked him to leave my house. Initially, he refused, claiming he had a right to be wherever his daughter was. When Justin finally approached the door, as if leaving, he cleared his throat, straightened his tie, and informed me that he would return in two days. Enraged by his arrogance and sense of entitlement to my home, I shouted a loud, "Fuck you!" then picked up the telephone to call a friend. When I looked up, Justin was walking toward me. Predicting his motions, I curled my head and chest over the baby, who was in my arms nursing.

I responded to the assault by filing a restraining order against Justin. It was a surprising and uncharacteristic move on my part; I was more accustomed to self-destruction than self-protection. It was also incredibly empowering. In one fell swoop, I decided to defend myself, against Justin and everything else that was weighing me down.

———◆———

ON APRIL 29, 1992, I woke up shaking and sweating as dawn was breaking. Nearly every night since the year began I had been taunted by a recurring nightmare. In the mornings, I scribbled as many details as I could remember. It was always the same. The sight of flames burning secrets, burning flesh like ebony wax, the buzz of whispering voices relaying cryptic messages. *Wednesday's child is full of woe*, my younger sister, Paula, would always say in the dream.

That particular morning I didn't bother trying to decipher the dream. I got up, shook the fear out of my bones, and promised myself a productive day. Productive meant writing, something I hardly did anymore. My life revolved around cleaning, pureeing vegetables, folding laundry, taking care of Korama, watching TV, and teaching two creative writing classes each week. By midday when I put Korama down for her nap, I decided I was too drained to step into a poem. It would just have to wait till another day.

Plopping myself down on the bed, I clicked on the small black and white television, tuned into the courtroom channel, and eased into a state of mindlessness. The verdicts from the Rodney King trial were announced minutes after I turned on the TV. The officers accused of using excessive force on Rodney King had been found "not guilty." My first reaction was one of absolute terror.

I picked Korama up and held her sleeping body close to me as if that was all it would take to protect her, or me, from the prejudice in this world. We, all black people, had just been told that our lives were of no value, especially in the hands of white justice. Earlier that month, Korama had celebrated her first birthday. All I could think about was that I didn't want her to grow up knowing the pain of racism, the pain of the despair it creates. I didn't want her to ever think of herself as that dirty word—*nigger*. The first time I was called a nigger to my face was at a boarding school mixer. I asked a white boy from one of the visiting schools to dance.

"No thank you. I don't dance with niggers," he answered politely, as if I had asked him what time it was.

"What'd you say?" I was bewildered.

"I said, no thank you, miss," he repeated and stepped away. Even the way he said "miss" turned the title into a degrading slur, as if I was a servant who had offered him a tall glass of mint julep. Afterward, I felt like someone had sprayed sticky dust all over my body. I wanted to run back to my dorm room, jump in the shower, and scrub away the filth of his insult. Even now when I hear that word—*nigger*—whether it is spoken by a black person or a white person, it is the simple tone and disgust of that boy's voice that I hear.

Riots ensued shortly after the verdicts. There was anarchy in the streets. After Korama got up from her nap, I fed her and we spent the rest of the day playing and watching the news on TV. The death toll rose rapidly. I listened as the television reporters referred to the predominantly black crowds as "packs," "herds," words generally used to describe animals, not human beings. When I could take no more of this verbal assault, I turned off the set and nervously paced the floor of the bedroom. From one window I could see flames. I pressed my mouth to the pane as if to stop a wail and studied the steam spreading over the glass. When would Korama and I—when would any black people—ever be able to find peace or happiness in this world?

More than anything, I wanted to cry but the tears would not come. Everything was out of order, out of control. Maybe there was nothing, nowhere, no reality that was "better," "perfect." Maybe this life of happiness that I dreamed of, longed for, was a mirage I had invented to decorate a cruel, barren world. If so, then why bother? Why bother to chase the unattainable? Why bother to keep on living a lie?

This is how the world feels to me when I am depressed. Everything is blurry, out of focus, fading like a photograph; people seem incapable of change; living feels like a waste of time and effort, like a mad dash to nowhere. Sometimes I get the sense that I am running so fast, too fast, so far ahead of myself, and I am always trying to go back, fall into the memory of a time that traveled too fast to touch. That night, like the night of my high-school mixer, I wanted so desperately to cleanse myself of everything that was happening. How wonderful it would be if I could jump in a shower and scrub away the isolation and the rage. If only I could watch the filth of the two years that had just passed slide down a drain and disappear forever.

Justin was as far out of my life as he would ever be. After I filed the restraining order, he filed one also, claiming that it was *I* who had physically attacked *him*. The judge granted us a mutual restraining order. Since that night he beat me, the only times I had seen Justin were in courtrooms where we both sat, mute and motionless, as our attorneys haggled over the details of custody, support, and visitation. I was thrilled to be able to move him to the edge of my life, but something told me that it was not really over, that at any given minute our saga would continue. The other shoe was bound to drop.

I felt a tickling sensation on the inside of my right thigh. I peeled my lips away from the window and looked down, expecting to find Korama standing beside me, her thin nails grazing my flesh. But she was across the room fast asleep again on her activity blanket. Perhaps, I thought, it was an insect. I reached down to swat it off. When I lifted my housedress and touched my hand to my thigh, I discovered it was my own blood gliding smoothly down my leg.

I was still breastfeeding, but my menstrual cycle had been fairly regular for the last three or four months. It was not due for another week and a half. The blood, which had made its way down to my ankle, was thick and it glowed against the palm of my hand. Unmoved, I stared out the window again, tried to see through the grey smoke that masked the sky. The moon was nowhere to be found. I closed my eyes and listened to the sirens and the sounds the helicopter propellers made as they shaved the clouds. A change was definitely coming into our lives.

There was so much to be angry about. There was so much that was uncertain except that for once, I was not alone. If only for one night, I knew there was no shortage of discom-

fort and agony in the city. Many black women were marching the streets, bearing arms, battling men, battling each
other, dressing the dead, aching in their wombs. In one way
or another, we were all suffering. Mine would not be the
only blood to be shed.

Before going to bed, I popped a cassette into the tape
recorder. It was a medley of songs I had recorded specifically for use in the hospital delivery room. I was cold but I
stayed on top of the covers. The sound of Billie Holiday's
voice in the first song that played spread through the room
like molasses. I began quilting together the best of my
remembrances and consoling myself with their warmth.

> willow weep for me
> willow weep for me
> bend your branches down
> along the ground and cover me
> listen to my plea
> hear me willow and weep for me

Hearing Billie conjured the tears I had been needing
to release all evening. And how sweet those tears were.
Almost as sweet as the round-mouthed kisses Korama
used to flood my cheeks with before she learned how to
pucker. Almost as sweet as the time my sister, Paula,
and I celebrated my first New Year's Eve in California at
Disneyland, or the pre-college weekends when my best
friend, David Hatcher, and I used to hang at Pizzeria
Uno in Georgetown drinking mugs of cheap beer, acting

worldly and sophisticated. Those tears were as sweet and welcome as anything that has ever assuaged my spirit.

Billie's voice was thick and husky. She carried the tune of my worries gracefully. Since I had been living in Los Angeles, I hadn't noticed any willow trees. I stopped searching for them when I left Washington, D.C. On a Sunday afternoon when I was about ten, my mother's older brother, Uncle Paul, took me out for a drive. He taught me the names of all the flowers and trees and plants we saw along the way.

Of all the trees and plants Uncle Paul pointed out that day, the weeping willow was the only one that stayed with me over the years. It struck me as odd and unfair that a tree so beautifully delicate and regal like the willow should be forever associated with tears. Who had come upon it and decided for us all that it should be a universal symbol of sadness? From that day forward, each time I saw a willow tree I wished it and all who had wept beneath its branches joy. I thought to do this not because I didn't know profound sadness at ten. As young as I was, I knew it well. It was that I believed such sadness could be overcome.

> gone, my lovely dreams
> lovely summer dreams
> gone and left me here
> to weep my tears along the stream
> sad as I can be
> hear me willow and weep for me

How ironic that years later I would be lying in bed wishing along with Billie Holiday for that same tree to affirm my sorrow, one that I wasn't sure I would ever overcome. I had been swinging in and out of sadness so briskly for the last couple of years I could hardly remember a time when it was not the norm. A time like that did exist for me though. I had been happy before. Keeping that in mind, it became imperative to try to find my way back to the person I had been inside that emotion.

HOME

———

———◆———

*Women run away because they must. I ran because if
I had not, I would have died. No one told me that
you take your world with you, that running becomes
a habit, that the secret to running is to know why you
run and where you are going—and to leave behind the
reason you run.*

—Dorothy Allison

from *Two or Three Things I Know for Sure*

THE MORE AFRAID I was of the future, the tighter I clung to the past, however distorted or romanticized my re-creation of it might have been. Shortly after the riots, I decided to move back to Washington, D.C. It appeared to be the most practical thing for me to do. There was nothing left for me in L.A.

Korama and I arrived in D.C. on a typical June day. The weather was so hot and humid people walked around simmering in their sweat. And there were so many people in such a small amount of space. I had almost forgotten how it felt to be in a crowded East Coast city. When I welcomed the wide-open spaces and perfectly manicured neighborhoods of Los Angeles, D.C. life, with its sultry summers and insipid bureaucrats, had seemed oppressive to me; it was one of my least favorite places. Shortly after turning eighteen I fled from that city and from my family—especially my family—with little more than a pledge to never return.

But there I was, completely unconcerned about any of that. Whatever hardships I had been through in this city were fully absorbed by the thickness of my nostalgia. When I stepped out of that airport into the heat and hustle-bustle of the Nation's Capital, it felt nurturing; it felt very right. An old school friend met us at the airport. The drive to Mum's house was long but stimulating. I lingered in the déjà vus brought on by street names and buildings. Some things seemed only vaguely familiar while others invoked vivid pictures. I made a mental list of all the things I would do and all the people I would call once I got settled. So many changes had been made to the city in my absence. I was eager to explore and rediscover the place. It was like having a fresh start.

Mum had moved out of the apartment where I spent my adolescent years. She and Paula were living in The Ivy, a master-planned community of apartments and tract houses in some jerkwater portion of the outer suburbs. Each building in the complex resembled the next. It was like someone had made a million carbon copies of their dream home. The community was generously bestowed with tall corn fields and cow pastures. It was rather charming and quaint. If nothing else, The Ivy would be my haven.

Much of the first couple of days I was back were spent

doing and seeing very little. Even if I had wanted to, it was nearly impossible to leave The Ivy unless you had your own vehicle, which I did not. There were a few bus lines that ran in the general direction of The Ivy but the stops were a half-mile or so away, past the cornfields—and none of the trails leading to them were paved. It seemed that the community was still in the midst of development. After I had been living there for a month I came to view its inaccessibility as some sort of corporate scheme concocted to discourage prospective residents from a lower income level (i.e., those people who relied solely on public transit) from moving there. Anyway, The Ivy, like all my other havens before it, became a prison.

It had been so long since I lived with my family that, at first, they treated me like a house-guest. I took a vacation from all responsibility, lying in bed while Mum cooked, Paula cleaned, and the two took turns tending to Korama. It was the first time ever that I had help with the baby. That lack of parental obligation gave me much-needed space and time, both of which facilitated another depressive episode, which my mother mistook for laziness. Depression is frequently mistaken for indolence. Needless to say, the novelty of my presence wore off quickly. Mum and Paula went back to their usual routines and I was left to create yet again another new life for my daughter and myself.

Even under the best of circumstances it can be disheartening for an adult to live under her parent's roof no matter how kind or well-intentioned the parent or the "child." The relationship between Mum and me regressed. Old wounds reopened; we found ourselves engaging in arguments that had already been fought, reviving resentments that had been laid to rest. These were not the memories of home I had conjured when I was in Los Angeles. But those depression-induced memories were not at all representative of what day-to-day life used to be for me. They were just isolated events and unrealistic portraits of tranquility I had drawn based on the need to climb back into a few frozen moments of joy.

There was a shared unhappiness in the household. I couldn't figure out whether it was merely another piece of luggage I had carried with me or whether it existed prior to my arrival. Either way, it was there, tight and unyielding, with a life and rhythm all its own. It was what held our lives together. But even the word "together" suggests a certain level of sharing. The three of us rarely shared anything other than the house and its facilities. Each of us went her separate way in the morning, came home, ate alone or in the company of a television set, and then disappeared behind her bedroom door.

I drank a lot in those days. Since alcohol is a depressant, the drinking only worsened my condition. I wasn't aware of this then. Chances are, even if I had been, it wouldn't have mattered. Alcohol was my home remedy, an ointment to rub into my wounds. The immediate effects of drinking were gratifying.

The more I stayed with my family and shrank into myself, the more my nostalgia faded. I remembered with complete clarity that this was the way I had felt while I was growing up. Whatever depression I brought with me from L.A. was simply the same one I had been trying to run away from when I first left home.

Eventually, I hired a babysitter and registered with a temp agency in D.C. As was true of my life in L.A., the bulk of my time went to working, mothering, and staying in bed. Although I had initially looked forward to renewing old friendships, the conversations I had with the friends and schoolmates who still lived nearby discouraged me from seeking their company. It was like adolescence all over again. Not much had changed in their lives. Most of them were still living with their parents, loitering at McDonald's, cruising the same bars, and spreading the same gossip. The thought of living with my mother and hanging with the old gang was torturous. I had no idea what I was doing with my life beyond the next five minutes, but I knew I didn't want to return to that way of life. The misery was all-consuming and I wanted to get out of it, but there was no place else left for me to run.

I no longer had the recurring nightmare of flames and heat. My dreams now were filled with water. And I was cold all the time—in the middle of July. It was a bone-biting kind of cold, the kind that doesn't go away no matter how many blankets you cover yourself with. In my dreams there was always a drowning child that I had to save. I didn't know who the little girl was but I sensed that I was her only hope. Her survival was in my hands. Me, who could barely save myself. Fear would rush through my limbs as I called out for help. There was never anyone else around, no one to save her in my stead. *Help her!* I'd scream. *Somebody please! Help her! I can't do it! I can't do it!*

I would start my day, every day, with the feeling of failure, with the knowledge that the life of some small child had been placed in the palms of my hands, and that without some miraculous intervention, there was very little I could do for her, or for me.

By then I vaguely knew—although I was not ready or willing to admit it—that I was clinically depressed. Before I left L.A., a friend of mine, Eugene Bledsoe, had even told me so.

During the time of the riots, Eugene and I struck up a long-distance friendship. He was thirty-five, a staff writer for a Minnesota newspaper, and a frequent freelancer to several national magazines. A mutual friend had recommended Eugene to me for a writing project I was working on, so I called him. Even though we had never met, we became best buddies almost immediately. Not a day went by without one of us phoning the other.

Over a short period of time, Eugene "watched" me go through many emotional upheavals. Finally, one day when I was telling him about some of the problems I was having, he said, "Meri, it sounds like you are severely depressed." His statement came as a complete shock. If he had just said he thought I sounded depressed, I think I would have been able to handle that because the word, depression, is thrown about casually to describe moods that are relatively normal in the scale of human emotions. What I found distressing was that he qualified it as *severe*.

"Severely depressed?!?" I responded. "Me?!? What are you talking about? What would make you think that?"

"It seems pretty obvious to me," he said. "You claim you can't sleep at night and that you have no appetite, you stay cooped up inside all day and, quite frankly, your attitude sucks. I mean, Meri, it makes sense, doesn't it? You've been through a lot of shit. You didn't think you'd just come out on the other side and that everything would be okay, did you?"

I was beyond bothered by Eugene's insinuation that I hadn't "come out on the other side" of the difficult situations I had just faced. Considering the circumstances—a high-risk pregnancy, poverty, domestic violence, single motherhood—I thought I was doing pretty well. After all, I wasn't on welfare, I wasn't smoking crack or abusing my child.

"Yeah, Gene, I did think so. And anyway, who made you the expert on *severe* depression?"

"My mother," he said with a laugh. "She's suffered from it for over thirty years."

"What?!" I asked, not believing what I had just heard. "Patricia Bledsoe? *The* Patricia Bledsoe?"

By sheer coincidence, Eugene had also been raised in Washington, D.C. His mother, Patricia Bledsoe, was a prominent person in D.C.'s black middle class. I didn't know her, but I certainly knew of her. She had worked closely with many local and national politicians.

"The one and only," Eugene said casually.

"Why would *she* be depressed?" I wanted to know.

"I'll tell you all about it later," he said.

Later arrived fairly quickly. During the last week of July, Eugene came to D.C. to promote his recently published book. I went to see him at his parents' home, a four-level brick house in the same serene neighborhood where my Uncle Paul used to live, where I had seen my first willow tree. It was our first in-person meeting. When Eugene opened the door, I wasn't surprised at all by what I saw. He looked exactly like I had pictured him in my mind— broad-shouldered, average height, brown-skinned, and extremely clean-cut, like a conservative company man.

But Eugene's mother took me by great surprise. I was expecting her to be old, feeble, and withdrawn, what I imagined someone who had been depressed for over three decades would look like. She was the exact opposite. She stood a little over five feet, was absolutely beautiful, and full of energy. If life had ever been unkind to her, it didn't show. There was not a hint of resignation on her face or in her spirit.

"Eugene," I whispered, "this is not a depressed woman." He shrugged his shoulders.

"Yeah, well, it's summertime. Catch her in six months."

Fall and winter, Eugene told me, were generally the only times his mother suffered from depression.

"Every fall and winter?" I asked.

"Pretty much," he said. Then, after much prodding, he told me the story of her long-time battle with depression.

As the result of a condition called Seasonal Affective Disorder (SAD), Patricia Bledsoe's depressions are cyclical. Her SAD symptoms appear in the fall and gradually disappear in the springtime. Dr. Norman E. Rosenthal, a trailblazer in the study of SAD (who also suffers from the disorder) writes in his book *Winter Blues* that "States of mind evoked by the seasons and the weather form a part of our language. A person is said to have a 'sunny disposition,' a 'radiant smile,' to be 'warm,' or 'cold.' . . . The weather and the changing seasons affect the way many of us feel, how we sleep, what we eat, whether we can concentrate on our work, and even whether we are able to love.

". . . Artificial methods of escape from darkness, cold, moisture, and extreme heat have provided us with considerable protection from the effects of the seasons on our bodies, minds, and spirits. With this protection, the changing seasons are for many people merely the backdrops against which to go about their daily business. But others experience them with extreme intensity."

———— ◆ ————

PATRICIA BLEDSOE'S FIRST encounter with a major depressive episode took place in the fall of 1960, when she was twenty-eight.

"It was a very distinct feeling, like nothing I had ever experienced before," she explained to me when I finally got up the nerve to ask her about her illness.

"I was racked with an excessive amount of guilt. I would sit all day and think of all the horrible things I had ever done in my life. I couldn't even make simple decisions like whether to eat cornflakes for breakfast or oatmeal, if I should go to the bathroom when I needed to or hold the urge a little bit longer."

A month after Patricia gave birth to Robert, the youngest of her three children, she suffered a stroke that left her in a coma for several days. When she came out of the coma, she went through physical therapy. A few weeks after her release from the hospital, she and her husband, Gilbert, were getting dressed to go to a political function. Patricia sat on the couch and started crying. She asked her husband why he didn't just let her die in the hospital. Both he and the children, she told him, would probably be better off if she were dead.

"It was just so unlike me to be that negative," she said. "After that evening all hell seemed to break loose."

Patricia developed an obsession with cleanliness and death. Those were the two things that occupied her thoughts. Assuming that the feelings she was experiencing were aftereffects of the stroke, Patricia went to her neurologist for help. He ran a series of tests. The results indicated that nothing physical was wrong with her. The neurologist, a white doctor, suggested that Patricia see a psychiatrist.

"Did the psychiatrist put you in therapy?" I asked.

"Therapy?" she said with a smirk. "I was so offended when that white man referred me to a psychiatrist. I thought he was telling me I was crazy because he didn't want to be bothered with me anymore. You have to remember, this was the early sixties. I wasn't about to go to see a psychiatrist. Even white folks weren't doing that then, at least not like they are now. What I did do was go to some of the black doctors in town to see if they could find out what was wrong with me."

At the time, Patricia and her family lived in Lansing, Michigan. Prior to her stroke, she had been doing a lot of local civil rights work and was very active in various political circles. Knowing this, one of the doctors she went to told her that her distress was probably just a reaction to the war going on in the Congo.

"He told me I had Lumumba fever," she laughed. "Another doctor said I had housewives' syndrome. He told me to get a job, said it would make me feel better."

Patricia went through three years of being depressed during every autumn and every winter before she finally found a doctor in the black community who took her complaints seriously.

"His name was Dr. Clayton. He was a popular doctor in town. People liked him because he was just a regular kinda guy. When I went to see him, I was at the end of my rope. I told him that if somebody didn't do something to help me right away, I was going to kill myself. It had gotten that bad. Dr. Clayton said, 'Girl, don't you kill yourself in here, it'd be bad for my business.' But he wasn't like the others, he understood what I was saying and he really tried to help me."

Dr. Clayton took Patricia to the Michigan Mental Health Hospital and transferred her into the care of Dr. Thorpe, a white psychiatrist. She was admitted into the hospital, where she was then given a series of electroshock treatments and prescribed an antidepressant, Elavil.

When Eugene first told me this story, I realized that there was much of it that mirrored my own, but I couldn't bring myself to admit or accept that I, too, was clinically depressed.

Over a year later, when I sat down with Mrs. Bledsoe and listened to her tell the story, I had pretty much come to terms with my depression; yet there was still a part of me that didn't want to believe that either of us was or had ever been depressed. I considered the possibility that both of us had somehow been misdiagnosed. Of course, I know that we weren't; all the facts were staring me straight in the face. But, as Veronica Chambers points out in her memoir, *Mama's Girl*, "Black women are masters in emotional sleight of hand. The closer you get, the less you can see."

IN EARLY SEPTEMBER, just before my twenty-fifth birthday, I moved into my own place. It was a two-bedroom basement apartment in the Mt. Pleasant section of town. I decided to live in Mt. Pleasant because it was near the National Zoo, which I thought would be exciting for Korama. An added plus was that Bryan Dunning, a friend I had met in Los Angeles, also lived in the neighborhood.

At first, I thought it rather chic to be living in the refurbished basement of a brownstone, but had I been asked to describe my apartment after living there for six weeks, chic would have been the least appropriate word. All of the overhead lighting was fluorescent. There were only three small windows in the entire place, so it got very little natural light. I felt like a caged laboratory rat. Since the brownstone was built on a slope, the front portion of the basement, where the bedrooms were, was completely subterranean. I had to walk down four huge concrete steps, beneath street level, to enter my apartment. It felt like I was going into a dungeon.

The mood in the apartment was so uninspiring, I forgot all about my plans to decorate and unpacked just the bare essentials. My computer and printer were set up on a huge cafeteria-style table in the largest of the two bedrooms, and I used the other room for storage. I put Korama's cot and my bed, a borrowed mattress and box spring, in the living room, where two of the three windows were.

It never occurred to me how drastically one's housing can affect one's mood. Living in that apartment taught me how essential it is for human beings to have a balance of nature, a constant stream of both natural light and natural darkness, in order to thrive. Now, not only do I live in a place that is full of windows and flooded with light, I have painted the living room in a bright shade of yellow so that the walls will catch and reflect the sun's rays.

Despite the situation with the apartment, all other aspects of my life were drifting into place. I was pleased with the overall progress I was making. One of my writing mentors, E. Ethelbert Miller, and I reconnected. Upon my return he gave me several employment leads. Through one of these leads I was contracted by the Smithsonian Institute as an independent research assistant for an upcoming exhibition. That assignment enabled me to create my own work schedule and paid enough money so I could enroll Korama in nursery school.

I started editing an anthology after the riots but had put it away when the depression became unmanageable. As soon as I got settled into my new place, I started working on the anthology again. A friend in Los Angeles shared my book idea with her literary agent who expressed interest in representing the project. I traveled to New York City for a meeting with the agent and we signed a contract to work together. Things were taking a turn for the better.

With each accomplishment my deflated self-esteem strengthened and soared. When I passed by store windows and caught a glimpse of myself through the corner of my eye, I couldn't help but smile because, all of a sudden, I liked what I saw. The nightmares stopped and I started sleeping soundly. I'd wake up early in the morning with a ton of energy and squint my eyes again and again to make sure what I was feeling was real, that all five senses were crisp and alert. The worst of it is behind me, I told myself. Moving back to D.C. had been a good idea after all. The change of scenery was doing wonders.

Eugene called during the first week of the "new," nondepressed me.

"Hello," I chirped into the phone.

"Meri?" he asked, in an uncertain tone, as if he had dialed the wrong number. I guess he had grown so accustomed to my hollow greetings the vibrant voice must have thrown him.

"It's me," I screeched. "Waz up, baaaaby??"

"Let me guess," he joked, "you just won the Publishers' Clearing House Sweepstakes prize."

"Don't I wish, Gene. I'd be in Disneyland right now. Hey,

what've you been up to lately? I feel like I haven't heard your voice in ages."

We spoke so frequently that a few days of us not talking felt more like a few months.

"Nothing. Just writing, hanging out. Meri, you sound great. Did something happen?"

"Nope. Nothing. Just the same ole same ole. What? A black woman can't be happy just cuz?"

Along with the new job, new apartment, and new me came a new set of friends. Scott Riley was the first person I befriended in the neighborhood. He lived three houses away. In the mornings when I walked Korama to nursery school, I would see him bopping up and down the street with his two huge dogs, a black Akita and a German Shepherd.

Scott was thirty-seven, short, blue-eyed, and balding, with a heavy Bronx accent. He was a recovering alcoholic/drug addict five years sober and he ran an environmental consulting company from his home. The first time Scott and I formally met, we sat on the stoop of my brownstone and had a lengthy conversation over a cup of coffee. We talked about our lives. I told him about Justin and explained that I had left L.A. because I needed a change of pace. He told me about the harsh twists of fate that had landed him in Mt. Pleasant.

He, too, it seemed, was in search of a new beginning. His mother, who was also an alcoholic, died when he was seven. His father, a zookeeper at the Bronx Zoo, remarried a heroin addict. Following in his father's footsteps, Scott studied zoology at the University of Colorado. He was to take a job at the Bronx Zoo after completing college, but by the time he returned to the Bronx, he was already a substance abuser. After he became sober, he moved to D.C.

About the same time that Scott and I became friends, I met Jade Parsons. Her cousin, Aaron, was a friend of mine in L.A. When he heard that I was moving to Washington, he gave me Jade's number and made me promise to get in touch with her. When I called her, I discovered that Jade had recently moved to the D.C. area from upstate New York, where she had been attending undergraduate school. While she was away at school, her parents had relocated to a Maryland suburb and were living in, of all places, The Ivy. Jade was twenty-six. We got along well and we had a lot in common. I would later find out that clinical depression was one of those things.

———◆———

IT WASN'T UNTIL late November, just before Thanksgiving, that my depression returned. As autumn made way for winter, the amount of light my apartment received steadily decreased. The first changes were in my eating and sleeping habits. I wasn't doing either. This, of course, affected my productivity. My contract deadline with the Smithsonian was just around the corner. I hadn't done very much work on the project. When I was first hired, I looked forward to spending my afternoons sifting through books, magazine articles, and newspaper clippings to find information that would be useful for the exhibit.

Soon, the trips to the libraries and archives became frustrating. I came up with a million reasons to stay home in bed. I didn't want to leave my house to walk to the bus stop; the weather was too chilly. It was annoying to be in the presence of so many people on the buses, on the trains, in the buildings. On those days that I was able to force myself to go to the library, my mind was so clouded that I would spend an unreasonable amount of time reading a single article and then immediately forget what I had just read. Searching through the microfiche to locate information was enough to drive me to tears. The words on the screen were so tiny and they looked like they were jumbled too tightly together; breaking them up so I could find what I was looking for was frustratingly strenuous.

One symptom produced another. I developed insomnia, then guilt over my inability to work. I blamed my lack of productivity on the insomnia, and I blamed the insomnia on my newly expanded social life. I had gone out drinking several times with Jade and her friends; Scott spent an hour or two each day at my house; Bryan stopped over nearly every night on his way home from work; and Paula spent every other weekend at my apartment.

On top of all that, I continued to have my daily telephone sessions with Eugene *and* was actively involved with Korama—above and beyond my normal parental duties. I arranged frequent play dates for her with other children; a few times a week, Bryan and I took her to the park or the zoo. With all this activity, who had time to sleep, let alone work? My determination dwindled.

"Are you going into a depression again?" Eugene asked one evening. He was still hell bent on making me come to terms with the fact that I was depressed. I was still grasping at straws to find another reason, any reason, other than depression, to explain my periods of "down time."

"Again? That would be impossible, Gene. I've never been in a depression before. I just need to slow down. I've been pushing myself too hard."

"Yeah, you do sound tired. You should probably get some rest. I'll call you tomorrow."

Even though I went to bed at nine o'clock that night, I wasn't able to fall asleep until dawn. I tried everything— warm milk, reading, watching TV. Nothing worked. The warm milk irritated my stomach. I finished a whole novel and then watched TV until the screen was filled with snow. It seemed like I had been asleep for no longer than five minutes when Korama poked at my eyelid with her index finger.

"Mommy, open the eyes. Open the eyes," she cried. I opened my eyes but was too drowsy to get up. Her toys were on the carpet next to the bed. I reached down, scooped up a handful, and tossed them next to me on the mattress. She climbed over me, sat in front of the toys, and sucked her thumb.

I nodded in and out of sleep for what seemed like a few seconds but might very well have been an hour. The last time I woke up, I stared at her holding a doll with one hand and greedily sucking the thumb on her other hand. I felt ashamed and selfish. She needed to be fed, bathed, and taken to nursery school. As I prepared myself to get up, the phone started ringing. It was Eugene.

"Hey, Meri. Just checking on you. I wanted to see how you're feeling."

According to the numbers flashing on the alarm clock, it was two. I knew that couldn't be the correct time. One of the many ways I con myself into waking up is by strategically placing several alarm clocks around my room, far enough away from my bed so I have to actually get up to turn them off. I also set them by as much as three, four, sometimes five hours ahead of the correct time. Usually, I am too groggy in the mornings to do the arithmetic, so I just get up.

"God, Gene," I grumbled. "Why are you calling so early in the morning? What time is it anyway?"

"Almost eleven. You're still in bed? I thought you were going to turn in early last night." Eugene was the perfect journalist, always prying, trying to stab out any bit of information he could get.

"I did," I said, yawning. "But I couldn't get to sleep. Can I call you back later?"

"No," he replied in a stern voice. "You can't. Get up and get dressed. You shouldn't stay in bed all day."

"Do you mind?" I screamed into the receiver. "What are you now, my father? I have—" He cut me off.

"A bad attitude and a serious case of depression."

I was too tired to argue or get defensive. Truthfully, I was flattered by his protectiveness. It was nice to know that somebody cared. I sat up.

"Alright already. I'm up. I'm up. Geez." I tore the covers

off of me and stood up. "You know, Eugene," I said in a creaky voice. "I think you've lost your mind."

"Well, better me than you, right? Take a walk or something. The fresh air might help you. I'll check back with you later."

"Take a walk. The fresh air might help," I repeated in a mocking, nasally voice as I dragged myself into the kitchen to start making breakfast. "Fresh air my foot," I screamed at the toaster. "It's freezing in this stupid city."

The day had barely begun and already it was shot. It was way too late to take Korama to nursery school. As a rule, they didn't accept children after ten-thirty. She would have to stay home with me the entire day. I looked over at her. She was still sitting quietly on the bed. She looked like a wounded puppy—sad, pained, waiting for help. I wanted so badly to be a good mother to her. All she had was me, and the weight of that responsibility was almost as heavy as the burden of my depression. I didn't want to take care of anybody else. I didn't even know how to take care of myself. All I wanted to do was crank up the heat and get back under the covers.

After Korama and I ate breakfast, I ran the water for her bath. As soon as I put her in the tub, the phone rang. It was Eugene again.

"Just wanted to make sure you were up and about," he said. I couldn't believe he called back.

"I said I'm up already. I don't need to be monitored. Leave me alone." I was angry but my voice was too hoarse to hold any power.

"I love you too, Meri," he said before hanging up.

I ran back to the bathroom and watched Korama play with her tub toys. The phone rang again.

"Back off, Eugene," I hollered into the receiver.

There was silence on the other end.

"Meri," a voice finally said. "Is everything alright?" It was Jade.

"Oh, Jade," I laughed. "I'm sorry. I just hung up with somebody and I assumed it was him calling back."

"Sounds like you're in the middle of something intense. Do you want me to call you later?"

"Nope," I said. "I can talk for a minute or so."

"Okay. You'll never guess what I just got." She must have been certain about that because she didn't give me a chance to try. "A car! I finally have a way to escape from The Ivy. I'm gonna drive into the city later on and I was wondering if you wanted to go for a ride, maybe get some dinner."

I was excited for Jade. I knew all too well how it felt to be stuck out in the boondocks of The Ivy. Her invitation was tempting but I knew I needed to spend time with Korama. There was so much housework and Smithsonian work to do. The clock was ticking dangerously close to my deadline. My whole day was going to be devoted to playing catch-up. The way I was feeling, the last thing I wanted to do was be out in public.

"Naw, but I'll take a rain check. I kinda want to stay home. I'm not really up for being around a bunch of people. But congratulations on the car."

"I hear you. I'm in that same space. Unfortunately, home for me is a group situation." She sounded disappointed.

"Listen, since I'm gonna be in your area anyway, can I still stop by for a few minutes to say hi? It'll just be me, and we don't have to go anywhere or do anything."

I took a moment to respond. If Jade was going to come over, that meant I would definitely have to bathe and clean up the house.

"I guess," I said hesitantly. "I doubt we're gonna go anywhere today. But I gotta warn you, my place is a mess."

"I don't think it's any messier than my room. I'll see you around five."

I spent the entire afternoon playing with Korama. It was my way of compensating for my inattentiveness that morning. After both of us were good and tired, I put a movie in the VCR, cleaned up, and decided to lay down for a short nap before working. Just as I put my head down on the pillow, the phone rang yet again. It was Paula.

"Nana-Ama," she said, calling me by my Ghanaian name. Her voice was a wind above a whisper.

"Paula? I can barely hear you." She spoke louder.

"Can you hear me now?"

"It's a little better," I said. "Is something wrong, Pooh?" I had given Paula that pet name when she was two years old.

"No," she sniffled.

"Have you been crying?" There was no reply. "Paula? Are you still there?"

"C-c-can I move in with you?"

I gathered that she and Mum were in the middle of an argument.

"Why?" I asked. "Not that I don't want you here but—" A beep tone sounded, indicating that there was another call waiting on the line. "Hold on. I've got another call. Don't hang up, okay?" It was Mum.

"Nana-Ama, your sister . . ." She was rambling so fast and furious I didn't think I could get a word in.

"Mum . . . Mum . . . MUM. I have to call you back. Bye." She still hadn't stopped talking but I clicked back to Paula anyway.

"Okay, what's going on over there?"

"That was her wasn't it? I could hear her talking on her line. What'd she say?" I sat up and bunched the covers around my waist. I really need to start screening my calls, I thought to myself. As strange as it sounds, the answering machine is one of the many tools I now use to combat depression. I came to the decision that my emotions were far too delicate to be randomly subjected to the negativity and drama that phone calls from family and friends sometimes bring.

"Nana-Ama, I don't really feel like talking about it. Can I just spend the weekend there? Keiko and I were thinking about going shopping in Georgetown tomorrow. She can just meet me there."

"That's fine," I said.

Secretly, I was thrilled that Paula hadn't wanted to talk about whatever problems she and Mum were having. Refereeing their arguments required patience and objectivity, both of which I lacked. Now that we were living in the same city, I got the sense that Paula expected me to step completely into the big sister role, something that intimidated me.

Ten years apart, we had each grown up feeling like an only child. When Paula was four, I left home for boarding school. I returned two years later to attend the local public school but the year after I received my diploma, I moved to another state. Paula was the one member of my family that I made an effort to stay in close touch with. We wrote letters, talked on the phone and, when I could afford to, I sent for her. We were very close, but being a sister from three thousand miles away was very different than being a sister from thirty miles away.

I was cautious of my relationship with Paula because my parents had always been wary of my influence on her. They considered me the "black sheep" of the family, the fuck up. And, as far as they were concerned, with good reason. I had dropped out of college and moved clear across the country to do god-knows-what with god-knows-whom. They didn't want any of my bad life choices to rub off on Paula.

"Don't follow in your sister's footsteps," my father once warned her.

"She's a loser," Mum often reminded.

Talking to Paula about the pressures of her home life inevitably pushed me back into my own youth. I recognized that feeling of helplessness I sometimes heard in her voice. It reminded me of how I used to pray for someone to save me from my life. The closer Paula and I became the more I realized that guidance was not my forte, not when it came to her. I forced myself into believing that validating her experiences would only be an imposition of my past on her present.

She needs to learn to assess her own emotions, find her own strength, I told myself. She needs to fend for herself. So I gave her what I thought was enough space in which to do that without making her feel as though I was abandoning her. Which, in essence, is what I was really doing.

———◆———

DUSK IS MY least favorite time. I favor night over day, but when I watch the orange sun melting into the shadows of the sky, a ball of loneliness rolls down my spine. When Jade arrived, the sun was setting; I was beside myself with grief. There was no room inside of me for conversation or laughter. Normally, I steered clear of social situations if I felt myself dropping into a "mood," but seeing as how Jade was standing in my doorway, that wasn't an option. Fortunately, depression teaches you the fine art of multiplicity. You become adept at wearing the right mask for the right person on the right occasion. I shut my eyes for a second, inhaled deeply through my nostrils and braced myself like an actor preparing to go on stage. After I opened my eyes, I slid my mouth into a perfect Colgate smile.

"Jade," I said enthusiastically. "Are you still up for eating and taking a drive? I wouldn't mind getting out of the house. And it'll probably put Korama right to sleep."

"Yeah," Jade beamed, returning the bright smile I had just given her. Her driver's license was four weeks new. She grew up in Manhattan, pedestrian capital of the world, so she had never felt a pressing need to learn how to drive. That is, until she moved into The Ivy.

"I feel like I'm celebrating my sixteenth birthday ten years too late," she said as she helped me fasten the safety belt to Korama's car seat.

The three of us stopped at a nearby restaurant for dinner. And then we drove around in circles until we ended up on a small, windy road in Rock Creek Park. Korama was still awake in the back seat. We didn't secure her car seat properly so each time Jade made a turn, the seat toppled over in the same direction. Jade's driving left much to be desired.

She and I didn't talk at all. Whenever I turned up the volume on the radio, she turned it back down. "I can't concentrate," she'd snap. The streets along Rock Creek Park were dangerous and it was so dark I couldn't see well through the windshield. I started back-seat driving.

"Slow down," I'd yell whenever we hit a rough spot.

"Will you keep quiet?" she'd return.

Neither of us knew the city well enough to navigate along the back roads of the Creek. We got lost.

"Turn here," I'd advise.

"I think I should go straight," she'd demand.

"Go straight," I'd say.

"No, I think I should turn here," she'd protest.

We bickered and bickered until we landed in a narrow dead-end lane. I was afraid Jade wasn't skillful enough to reverse the car without dropping over the small cliff behind us or getting hit by a car coming from the opposite direction.

"Do you want me to turn the car around?" I asked.

"Just keep quiet, okay?" she warned. "You're making me jittery. I feel like I'm driving with my father."

Just as I was about to say something snide, I noticed that I wasn't apart from myself anymore. My mind wasn't tied up with Paula, Mum, or some self-deprecating thought. I was fully in that moment, to the point where I was actually enjoying it. I started laughing hysterically.

Jade was not as amused. She didn't say a word. She didn't even look my way. I couldn't tell if she was angry or just pensive. As we neared my apartment, the feelings of sadness and loneliness returned.

"You're a good driver," I told Jade. "I'm sorry about freaking you out."

It was a peace offering. I didn't want her to go away mad. I didn't want her to go away at all. Korama was fast asleep and would probably stay that way through the night. There was nothing waiting for me at home except a stack of books and a few beers. Jade did not respond to my apology. She pulled up to the stop sign at the intersection nearest to my apartment, put on her turn signal and waited for two pedestrians to cross the street. After they were safely on the sidewalk, she started to make her turn but she didn't drive far enough forward before cutting the wheel. The right tires of the car skipped over the curb.

"Oh shit!" she gasped.

Startled, the two pedestrians stopped walking and gaped at us. Jade completed the turn and carefully parallel parked the car in a spot directly in front of Scott's brownstone. She put on the emergency brake, removed the keys from the ignition, placed her foot on the seat, and leaned her back against the door so that she was facing me. She was biting her lower lip, holding back a smile.

"Now, what was that you just said about my driving?"

I looked at Jade and offered her a heartfelt smile. This was the most comfortable I had ever felt with her. She had an air of confidence that usually made me uneasy and insecure.

Neither of us made a move to get out of the car, nor did we feel compelled to chat. I rolled down the window and took a pack of cigarettes from my purse. Jade had never seen me smoke before. Few people had. It was a nasty habit that I tried to hide.

"Do you mind?" I asked.

"Not if you let me bum one."

I had never seen her smoke either. She rolled down her window and took a cigarette from the pack. I held the lighter to her cigarette then lit my own.

"I didn't know you smoked."

She blew a billow of smoke from the side of her mouth out the window.

"I didn't know you smoked either. I think there are a lot of things we don't know about each other," she said.

She took another puff.

"Can I ask you a personal question?"

I shrugged my shoulders.

"Sure." She lifted her other foot up onto the seat and wrapped her free arm around her legs, just below the knees.

"Are you depressed?"

The question didn't register.

"What did you ask me?"

She repeated it.

"Do you suffer from depression?"

There was a certain safety in her eyes that urged me to take a leap of faith.

"Yes," I heard myself say softly. "Yes, I think I do. Why did you, I mean, how did you—"

"I recognize the masks."

"I need a drink," I mumbled, walking into my kitchen. I had just finished moving Korama's cot into the room I used as a work area so that Jade and I would not disturb her. I grabbed two beers and went into the living room. Jade was rummaging through her backpack. She pulled out a tattered green notebook, flipped through its pages until she found what she was looking for. I handed her a beer.

"Here. Read this," she said, pointing to the page.

It was her journal. I sat down, placed the book on my lap and started to read. The entry was written in the summer, on Jade's birthday.

> I am twenty-six years old today and I look at my life. I feel as if I have nothing to show for my entire life but at the same time I recognize that that's not true and that all the work I have done in terms of overcoming my depression and remaining functional within society or even functional for myself has been a great feat. I guess it's dangerous

to read into the mainstream culture's definition
of what success is. But at this age I had anticipated
on being more, on having a lot more in my life. A
lot more in terms of my own sanity, my own personal peace. In terms of my own financial status,
my career, my own love for myself. Especially in
terms of school and right now I don't have any of
that. I am still not done with school. Ever since
grade school I have had problems with school.
And this is something that I am just now dealing
with. A great deal of the struggle has been in coming to terms with my depression. I have always
felt that I just wasn't strong enough. That there
was something wrong with me. I have always felt
that maybe God hated me and that he chose me to
carry a burden of pain for the rest of the world.
And I think the hardest part of overcoming, or at
least attempting to function within depression is
learning how to love myself. This year I will learn
how to love myself. I have to.

She had drawn a tiny heart at the end of the entry and
placed a question mark beside it. I closed the book, gave her
a hug.

"I don't know what to say."

"Do you feel that way, too?" she asked.

I didn't know how to answer so I returned her question
with a question.

"Have you learned to love yourself?"

She balled her hands into a fist.

"Sort of, sometimes." She cocked her head to the side, pounded the fist into her thigh. "How about you? Do you love yourself?"

"Yes," I lied. "Of course I do."

The look on her face said that she didn't believe me. I bowed my head and picked at my fingernails.

"Well," I went on without looking up, "I love the me that I have created, you know, the persona, this assertive writer-person that everyone likes. I love being her. As far as the me that I really am deep down inside, I don't know."

I raised my head, met her gaze.

"I really don't know how to answer that question, Jade. I don't know if I love myself."

I grabbed the pack of cigarettes.

"Want one?"

She nodded and helped herself. I lit her cigarette and took a swig of my beer.

"What medication are you on?" she asked.

I pictured myself lying in a hospital bed while a blank-faced nurse stood over me holding out a Dixie-cup full of pills.

"Medication?"

I got up to get an ashtray from the kitchen. Even though I had just admitted to Jade—and myself—that I suffered from depression, I suddenly found it difficult to accept the idea. I wanted to change my answer to "no," just like I had done on the hospital intake form. That's how deep my denial was.

"Oh no, girl," I laughed. "I'm not that far gone. There are days when I feel like you did on your birthday, like my life doesn't amount to much, but I hardly think that's cause for medication or a trip to the loony bin. Everybody gets that way sometimes, I suppose. I mean, I haven't had a nervous breakdown or anything."

The episodes I experienced in Los Angeles snuck into my mind, as did the emotional collapse I had when I first moved into my mother's home. I immediately cast them out and finished the point I was making.

"I mean, Jade, I'm just like you. We get down, we deal with it, we pick ourselves back up and we move on."

I put the ashtray on the floor. She rested her cigarette in one of the four grooves carved into its rim.

"I'm on Prozac," she sighed. "Forty milligrams a day."

Suddenly I felt embarrassed and frightened. People on Prozac were said to be unpredictable, even violent. On a television special I had seen, a man on Prozac had shot his wife and three children, then he turned the gun on himself. Another man had deliberately driven his car into a ravine. I wondered if Jade would get out of control. My heart was racing. What if she hurt me or Korama? The calmer part of my consciousness told me I was being paranoid. After all, she certainly had her chance to kill us all when we were on that dead-end road in Rock Creek Park.

"What . . . ," the words were stuck somewhere between my brain and my mouth. "W-w-what does the Prozac do? Does it, I mean are you, can you, h-h-how does it make you feel?"

She picked up on my anxiety and played with it.

"Like slicing my wrists. Got any razors around?"

The hair on my neck and arms stood straight. Jade laughed and touched my hand.

"It's alright, Meri. I'm not crazy. Well, no more than you."

She winked at me, pursed her lips, and picked her cigarette up from the ashtray.

My second wind caught up with me. The fear went away. It was as if I had entered my cool, calm, and collected persona. But I hadn't. I was still myself, the me that I am underneath the masks. From the first time Eugene suggested that I might be suffering from depression I knew he was right. Denying the truth seemed to me the most effective way to overpower it. What happened instead is that it consumed me. My every thought, my every move was either an affirmation (*"Why did I do/think that? That's how depressed people behave/feel."*) or a negation (*"See, I'm having fun. If I were really depressed, I wouldn't be having so much fun."*) of that truth.

Telling Jade that I was depressed did not leave me defenseless. Rather, it gave me a sudden surge of strength and determination. I wanted to know more.

"Tell me about your depression," I begged her. "When did you first realize you were depressed? What did you do? Does it ever go away for good?"

She went into the kitchen to get two more beers.

"Are you in therapy?" she shouted from the kitchen.

"No," I shouted back. When she returned to the living room, she sat down beside me and handed me a beer.

"When did *you* first realize that you were depressed?" Jade asked.

When did I? I scanned my life.

"I don't know. I've always been a sad person. I cry about the stupidest things. I cry at commercials, during cartoons, sometimes I cry about nothing at all. I cry for crying's sake."

"And you're not in therapy?"

"No way. I would never. Tonight was the first time I've ever told anyone. Well, my friend Eugene knew, but he figured it out on his own. He's been after me for months now to see a shrink. Someone in his family suffers from depression. Anyway, Eugene's convinced that my depression is clinical."

"As far as I'm concerned," Jade said, "all depression is clinical. People who are just having a bad day should use another word. They shouldn't say stuff like 'I'm so depressed because I failed a test' or 'I broke a nail and I'm depressed.' They're not depressed. They don't even begin to understand what real depression is."

"What is real depression? How did you know that's what you were feeling?" I wanted a concrete description from her. She swung her head back and studied the ceiling.

"How did I know? It's more like how did I not know? I knew before I knew, if you know what I mean. I was like you. I was always sad, always crying, always lonely, and nothing could change that. It was probably just my fate."

My spirits were waning.

"Do you think it will ever go away?" I asked. "Do you think that people like that, I mean, like us, can change the way we are?"

"Sure. I believe in change. But I don't know if I have the ability to change the fact that I have an illness."

Illness. It seemed like such a weighty word. Acceptance of my vulnerability to depression came in baby steps. Leukemia, cancer, heart disease, AIDS, even schizophrenia—*those* were illnesses. But depression? I wasn't buying it. Jade was slim and statuesque, with cinnamon-colored skin. Her hair was thick with tight, blue-black waves, and she wore it short, like a schoolboy. How could a woman so intelligent, so graceful, so *vibrant* describe herself as ill?

"Even if you were ill all of your life, there had to be one specific moment when you or someone else first realized it."

"There were a lot of those moments. Let's see, when was the first one? Since I was most likely born this way, I might as well start from day one." She lit a cigarette. "I was born in Cleveland. My mom got pregnant with me while she and my dad were on vacation in—"

"Wait a second," I said getting up. "I need to check on Korama. Let me do that now so I won't interrupt you later."

Jade used the phone to call home while I went into the back room. Korama was breathing deeply. Her mouth was open and the thumb she had been sucking was resting on her lower lip. It was cold in that room but she had kicked the covers off. I pulled them up over her body and tucked the sides under the mattress. When I touched her thumb to move it away from her face, she plugged it back into her mouth and sucked heartily without waking up. I went into the bathroom, threw cold water on my face, and watched in the mirror as it drifted down my cheeks and along my jawline.

"This is the face of a depressed person," I said to my reflection. "This is *my* face." I didn't know how to react to my own words. It was as if I had entered a trance. The whole evening was starting to feel surreal.

"Is everything alright?" Jade asked from the living room. Her voice pulled me from my reverie.

"Yup. All done," I said, closing the door behind me. Jade had swiped the comforter off the bed and wrapped herself in it. I sat across from her. She offered me part of the comforter. I pushed my feet under the cloth.

"I think I'm going to drop out of college again," she said, more to herself than to me.

"The photography class? Why? I thought you liked it."

"Depression. That's always the reason. That's why I'm living in The Ivy now. Remember I told you that I took a leave of absence from college? That's because my depression got really severe . . ."

There was that word again. *Severe.*

"What exactly do you mean by severe?" I asked.

"I mean being totally incapacitated. I had to drop out and move back in with my folks. It's funny, you know, when other people think of school, they remember things like being in a band or a play or getting good grades and awards. The things I remember are depression and therapy and feeling like I didn't belong. It's gotten in the way of everything I've ever wanted to be. At the rate I'm going, I'll never get through school."

She had a faraway look in her eyes, the kind people get when they lose themselves in themselves. Her eyes were shimmering but she didn't seem to be on the verge of tears. I propped my back against the wall, closed my eyes, and listened to her voice as if it was music, a sad, sad ballad.

"My mother says that I have always been timid and shy. As soon as we moved from Cleveland to New York, she put me in a nursery school. I hated going there at first. Whenever she dropped me off, I would sit in a corner and cry and cry and cry until she came to pick me up. Then I became friends with this girl, Susu. Her family was from Libya. They had just moved to New York. Susu and I used to share a mat during naptime. We used to go to each other's houses and play after school. I only knew her that one year but I still consider her the best friend I have ever had."

"What happened to her?" I asked.

"I don't know. After nursery school, I never saw her again. I guess she went to a different grade school."

"God," I yawned. "It's amazing that you can remember things from that far back. The past is one big blur to me."

"You'd be surprised how much you can remember if you try. The more I talk about my past in therapy, the more things I remember. I don't think you really forget anything. I think you just file it away for safe-keeping. If you concentrate long enough, everything comes back."

"Hmm," I shrugged. "I'm not sure I'd want to remember any of my past."

"Yeah," Jade laughed. "I know what you mean. I know what you mean."

"So what happened after you left nursery school?"

"Everything changed all at once. Kindergarten was okay, but I had a hard time making friends. I was so lonely that year. I really missed Susu. Then Monica was born. My mother and I had always been so close and then all of a sudden, there's this other daughter who she needs to pay attention to."

"Sounds like the initial stages of classic sibling rivalry to me," I teased.

"Yup," she agreed. "The seed for that was definitely being planted. Anyway, I got through that year okay. First grade was a nightmare though. But then, so was the rest of elementary school. It seemed like the older I got the worse the teachers got. And there weren't that many black kids in my elementary school so I couldn't even try to slip through the cracks. My grades, my attendance, my participation, everything about me stuck out like a sore thumb."

"I can relate to that. There weren't very many black kids in the schools I went to either."

"It was hard always being the only one. I had such a low self-image. In those days I used to think that if you touched the skin of a white person, it would make you lighter. Girl, don't you know I used to purposely brush up against those white kids when I passed them in the hallway? It was crazy self-hate."

"Top that with being a foreigner," I added. "It wasn't just white kids with me. It was everybody. I hated being different. I used to come home from school and stand in front of the mirror and practice talking like the kids in school, walking like them. Hell, I wanted to be them. All I knew was that I had to be someone other than who I was."

"I understand what you're talking about. I might as well have been a foreigner. It wasn't just about being white. It was about not wanting to be different. When I reached the eighth grade, I decided to change myself into a whole new person. I told myself, 'Look, I'm not going to be like this anymore. I am not going to be this shy, introverted loser anymore. I want to have people in my life.' So, I played at being outgoing. I would say hello to strangers in the hallway. I would speak up in class. I was playing at being happy and people responded to that. I loved it."

"Sounds just like someone I know," I giggled.

"Meri, after I did that one-eighty, I was all that. Pretty soon, I became one of the most popular kids in school. I met this girl, Julia. She was this white girl from the Lower East Side. She was sort of like a misfit too. She used to wear tight designer jeans and too much make-up. We started cutting classes. We'd hang out in Central Park drinking beer and smoking cigarettes. We were too fierce. Sometimes when we ditched school, she and I would meet at this arcade in Midtown and waste our lunch money playing Ms. PacMan all day. There was this one time when she was at the machine and I started to feel really claustrophobic, like if I didn't get out of that building, it would cave in and swallow me up."

"I get that way sometimes," I said. "All the colors and sounds start speeding around me in a circle, like I just got off a merry-go-round, except I'm standing on solid ground."

I closed my eyes and crossed my arms over my chest. Jade paused for a moment and took in what I said.

"It was something like that," she replied. "I ran out of the arcade and leaned against the brick wall near the entrance, but being outside didn't help. Julia came looking for me and asked me what was wrong. I told her the truth. I told her that sometimes I got this empty feeling inside, like I was just a shell and the rest of me was hollow. She held my hand and started crying. She said, 'Oh my God, Jade, I know what you mean. I feel that way too.' We just stood there hugging and crying for a long time.

"Later that night Julia called me. I had asked her to get the 411 on Jordan, this guy I liked. He was this jock who used to hang out with our crowd. Julia said that he thought I was a good friend but he would never date me because I was black. I was so hurt. I guess I was so used to going to school and being friends with all those white people, I thought I was an exception. You know, different, special.

"After I got off the phone with Julia, I laid down on my bed and tried to process everything. I was confused and hurt and pissed off and all those feelings were stuck in my throat. I felt like making myself throw up just to get those nasty feelings out of my body. It was as if I was in the arcade again. There wasn't enough air in the room. I couldn't breathe no matter how hard I gasped. I went out to the terrace and kept taking these deep breaths in and out. The whole time, there was this voice. Not like a human voice, more like a loud thought. It kept telling me to jump, just jump and put an end to it all."

I dozed off while listening to Jade's story. The words she was speaking merged with the dream I was having, the same dream I had been having for a while. *Jump, just jump*, a voice demanded. I was standing near a body of water. There was a little girl in the water. She was flailing her arms about, fighting with the water. She was drowning.

"Wait," I called out to the girl. "I'll find someone to help you."

The land by the water was lush, full of trees and plants and rocks.

"Help!" I screamed at the top of my lungs. "Somebody help!" There was no answer. No one was there except me and the girl. I didn't know what to do. My mind swelled with the temptation of evil. If I walked away, the responsibility of saving the girl would no longer be mine.

Jump, the voice insisted. I didn't know where it was coming from. It circled around me and hung in the air like mist.

"I can't jump in," I cried. "I can't do it. I don't know how to swim."

A warm hand with long, lean fingers grabbed my shoulder from behind and started shaking it. My head felt heavy, too heavy to turn.

"Meri, Meri," the voice called. I tried to turn my head.

"Meri, wake up." It was Jade's voice. "Meri, are you asleep? Wake up. Meri?"

I opened my eyes.

"Hmm? We have to save her. She's drowning. You go."

"Save who? Go where? You're falling asleep. Wake up."

I looked around. I could see my back terrace, the ashtray, my bed. I could see the empty green beer bottles lined up neatly in a row like bowling pins. Everything looked distorted. I squinted my eyes and strained to see clearly. There was no water, no trees, no child. I was in my home. Realizing this gave me little solace. I stood up and stretched.

"It's late," Jade said. "We should probably call it a night anyway. I've gotta be in the darkroom by noon."

The muscles in my neck were tight. It was still dark outside.

"I must have dozed off," I yawned. "I'm sorry. I didn't realize I was so tired. What time is it?"

She looked at her watch.

"It's four-thirty. Can I just crash here?"

I nodded my head. Fully clothed, we crawled on top of the mattress. Jade pulled the comforter from the floor and threw it over us. She cupped her cheek with her hand and sank her head into the pillow. Wide awake now, I lay facing the wall, with my back to hers. I thought about the dreams. The one of fire and the one of water. They weren't dreams at all. They were warped pieces of an old life haunting me. How could I have been so naive to believe that I could return to D.C. and create a future without contending with the past?

"Meri? Are you sleeping?" Jade whispered.

"Uh-uh," I replied, without parting my lips.

"What were you dreaming about? Who was drowning?"

"Me," I said plainly, as if I had known all along.

GHOSTS *at the* EDGE *of the* SWAMP

———

———————

Doesn't it always come down to its tokens—

the echoes of voice, the borrowed jewelry

of time,

the ghosts at the edge of the swamp

throwing petals on water?

—Gail Wronsky

from "She and I"

Again the Gemini Are in the Orchard

PAULA ARRIVED SHORTLY after Jade left. Her jaw was set hard, her stride was purposeful. She was tall, stick thin, radiantly dark, and disturbingly calm. Like our father, she rarely spoke and when she did, she gave the appearance of being in complete control. It was easy to forget that she was just fifteen. She was barely in the door when I asked her if she could stay with Korama for a couple of hours.

"Where are you going?" she wanted to know.

"I have to run an errand in Takoma Park," I said. "I know you're going to Georgetown with Keiko so I won't be long."

I was not so much running an errand as I was answering a calling. The exact spot where I was standing in my dream watching the child, myself, drown was behind an old brick building—702 Chaney Drive—in Takoma Park, Maryland.

There was a patch of woods there. And just beyond the woods was Sligo Creek. My family lived there from the summer before my eighth birthday until I was twelve.

On the days that I was feeling especially daring I would walk along the dirt trail that led to the water. In the time that we were living at 702 Chaney Drive, Paula was born, my parents separated, and I began to accept loss as an inevitable part of the life I would lead. Regardless of how much someone or something meant to me, I knew that I would lose it. After we moved from Chaney Drive, I never went back. Like everything else that had been dear to me, it was nothing more than a distant memory. I thought that if I went to the exact spot where the dream took place, I could maybe figure out what it meant.

After I left, I took a short-cut through the zoo to get to the subway station. The autumn wind beat my cheeks like a whip. I rolled my fisted hands into the pockets of my coat. Most of the coat's inner lining was shredded and both pockets had gaping holes. I kept curling and uncurling my fingers, gliding them around the slick fabric of the lining. The leaves crunched underneath my boots. I wondered what the weather was like in Los Angeles.

By the time I got to the subway platform, I couldn't feel my toes or fingers. My nose was running and my eyes were watery. I pushed my hands through the holes in the coat and rubbed them against the thick corduroy ridges on my slacks. The material felt hard against my numb fingertips. Thankfully, a train came right away. I was nervous about going back to my old neighborhood. The relationship I chose to maintain with my past was a very selective one. I knew the facts of my life well. Well enough to want to forget or rewrite the parts that were painful.

I exited the train at the Takoma Metro Station. I walked to the bus shelter where the Montgomery County's Ride-On Bus number 17 stopped. The breeze seemed more ruthless there than it had in Mt. Pleasant. It swept whatever litter and leaves were in its path. As the bus pulled away from the curb, I rested my head against the padding of the seat and prepared myself for what I was sure would be a shock.

Many names and skins have been shed in order for me to evolve into the person I now am. When I lived on Chaney Drive, my name was Mildred Brobby. The name on my birth certificate, which is hidden deep inside of some desk drawer in my home, is Mildred Mary Nana-Ama Boakyewaa Brobby. I was born in Accra, Ghana, on Wednesday, September 13, 1967. My mother left Ghana, and me, when I was three years old to attend Howard University. In Ghana, Mildred never was. The child that would become Mildred in the United States was called Nana-Ama. It was the name my friends and family used, the name that my grandmother who cared for me while Mum was away whispered into my six-year-old ears to comfort me as the plane carried us to America, to my mother.

My father joined us in America shortly after my arrival. Newly reconciled, my parents and I lived in an efficiency apartment in Washington, D.C. In the face of people who were not part of the culture that I had come to know as my own, my public name and, ultimately, my public persona became Mildred, the English name I was given at birth. My parents introduced me to every non-Ghanaian person as Mildred, which I imagined was the most ghastly name a person could have. It hung strangely on my bones, but it was what was given to me so I took it and absorbed all that it was until even my flesh became redolent of its ugliness.

Maybe it was the scent of insecurity and unattractiveness I was emitting, or it could have simply been the normal cruelty in which youth have been rumored to indulge, but I, and my name, became the target for incessant teasing and ridicule. I was called Mildew, Millicent, Silly Milly, Mil the Dreadful, and a host of other horrid epithets.

The children who sat behind me in class at St. Paul and Augustine, those innocent-looking children with "Hail Marys" in their eyes, unraveled the massive black strings that my mother hand-wrapped around my hair. They mocked my accent that refused to roll *r*s or clip vowels. They pinched their noses and slid away from me as I opened my lunch box. They told me I looked like a monkey, often referring to me as "the African Monkey," begging me to swing on branches and show them my tail.

When the bus turned onto Carroll Avenue, one of the main arteries in Takoma Park, a group of children dashed across the street, laughing and chasing one another. I could feel the heat of anguish rising through my chest, into my throat. The clatter of the children's laughter rang sweet and melodious in my ears, like the laughter of those cretins who taunted me in the Catholic school. It used to make me feel so rejected to hear them. How I wanted to join them in play, in laughter. If only they were not laughing at me.

Even when I was in Ghana I had been somewhat fragile, especially after my mother left, but these experiences in America shattered any personal pride I felt and replaced it with uncertainty and self-hatred.

When we moved to Takoma Park, I began attending a new school, Rolling Terrace Elementary, where the children were kinder. My father and I were especially close then. He took me everywhere with him. On school nights, he helped me with my homework. On Saturday mornings, he watched cartoons with me and in the afternoons, I watched wrestling and *Wide World of Sports* with him. Life made as much sense as it could to an eight year old.

Then Daddy started working late. Mum got pregnant and gave birth to Paula. Daddy worked later and later. There were loud discussions, arguments, and fights. Sometimes I could hear screaming, crashing, banging and breaking. Always breaking. The breaking of glass, the breaking of wood, the breaking of hearts. There was so much breaking. After Daddy left, Mum, Paula, and I lived in the apartment together, but what good is a home once it has been broken?

I got off the bus at the intersection of Carroll Avenue and Flower Avenue. On one side of the intersection was the Seventh Day Adventist Church. On the other was the Seventh Day Adventist Hospital, where Paula was born. With the exception of a traffic light dangling from a thick black cord in the air, not much had changed. I walked down

Flower Avenue until I reached Chaney Drive, a dinky dead-end road. 702, a nondescript four-story building, was at the very end of the street. The instant I saw it my memory gained strength.

The parking lot sloped out in front of the building like a sea of tar. I looked at the windows of our old apartment. When I stared through the open window of what used to be my bedroom, I could see myself, Mildred, vaguely in the shadows on the wall, my round face and dark brown complexion, those thick lips and chunky legs. Long after my father moved out, I used to sit by that window in the evenings, waiting for his car to roll into the lot, waiting for him to come back home. When night had finished falling and he hadn't returned, the despair cut so deeply, I thought it would slice me in half. This is the first clear memory I have of feeling overwhelmingly sad for a lengthy period of time, of hating myself so much that I wanted to die.

While I was sitting in my bedroom aching for my father, the music from the record player would slide under my closed door, like smoke. Usually, it was the song "I Will Survive," one woman's pledge to overcome the devastation of a break-up. Mum would play it over and over before she went to bed. Her grieving was systematic. Whenever I heard the song playing, I knew Mum was in the living room sitting on the couch. Or else she was furiously cleaning, scraping, and scrubbing appliances and counters as if she could, through the reflection of their crisp shine, catch a glimpse of the person she had hoped to become by then.

I, too, learned to welcome the soothing effects of nocturnal solitude. The kingdom of night was mine, and inside of it I discovered ways to reinvent myself. I sang, recited poems, and danced for the make-believe audience seated at the foot of my bed. Before daybreak, I would tune the small clock radio to my favorite sad song station and listen to the woeful words. How could a heart so young beat to the syncopated sorrows of such rhythms? Under the roof of the same home, there was a child crying like a grown woman in one room, a mother whimpering like a child in the other.

The wind was still blowing wildly; my fingers were still numb, pressing painfully into my palms. I walked around to the rear of the building and followed the dirt path to the creek. How many times had I wept beside that water? During one school recess at Rolling Terrace, a freckled-face redhead by the last name of Williams vowed to me that she would marry a man with a name that was higher up on the alphabet chain so she would not always be the last to be called on. The thought of changing my last name, Brobby, never occurred to me, but that conversation was significant because it made me realize that a person could rid themselves of an unwanted name. Right then, I knew that I would rid myself of Mildred.

For weeks I became fascinated with names, always paying special attention to introductions. This was an enchanting time because suddenly anything was possible. I could be called Elizabeth, like the queen, or Victoria, like the lake. Or I could be called India like the charcoal-colored girl in my class who was not from there but had hair that looked like shiny black ribbons. As I prepared to give a new label and identity to myself, I prepared also for the departure from Mildred, the self I so despised.

I convinced myself that only a plain, simple "American" name would provide me with what I wanted most desperately: the luxury of slipping into a void of invisibility. For this reason alone, Nana-Ama, the name I so loved, was not ideal. I chose, instead, to be known by my given middle name, Mary. Walking home from school one day with my blue canvas backpack slung across my shoulder, I noticed the messages that people had carved into trees. Some were initials of sweethearts. Some were bulletins of rage. I found the boldness of the authors intriguing. I wondered if I would ever have anything so urgent to say or make known that I would consider branding it into the face of nature. And if so, would I actually do it, or would I, characteristically, be too afraid?

Finally, I reached the scene I had re-created in my dream. It was the same place that I, as Mildred, had stood fourteen years before, listening to the water from Sligo Creek slap against the rocks, feeling the sweat trickle near my temples, cuddling a weathered slab of wood. I had found the wood on the way home from school, snatched it up off the ground, and stuffed it into my backpack. It was rectangular, about the size of my school notebook. With my eleven-year-old hand, I carefully spelled out my name on the wood board: M-I-L-D-R-E-D. After I had finished, I refused to allow my eyes to look at the crooked, unevenly dispersed letters.

I suspected that God was momentously present. God was there, watching. I thought about God's wrath, something I had heard so much of in Catholic school, about what punishments would be handed down to me for what I was about to do. That piece of wood was a tombstone of sorts symbolizing the death of "Mildred." But I was afraid to let go of it, afraid to wish for my own death, even if it was only in metaphor. I knew that once I put it down and walked away, I would never be able to go back to that place, that moment, the person I was leaving behind.

I have learned, with difficulty, that the need for separation cannot automatically be interpreted as rejection. Over the years, I distanced myself from the person I was as Mildred, the ugly little girl, the "monkey," the fatherless child. With twenty-five years of the world's grit under my nails, it finally got through to me that there was no way I could ever kill off whatever remainders of Mildred I carried inside of myself. Surely, finding the core reasons for the feelings I had learned to call "depression" meant saving Mildred, claiming my past, however traumatic.

I checked the time on my watch. I had been standing by the creek for far too long, nearly an hour and a half. I was cold; I was hungry. There was absolutely nothing I could do for the child that I once was.

"This is really stupid," I said out loud. "I can't change stuff that's already happened."

I decided to head back to Mt. Pleasant, make myself a big cup of cocoa, sit down with Korama and Paula, and warm myself with their love.

———◆———

A SLOW, STEADY FLOW of the events that took place in my childhood spilled from my mind during the bus and train rides home, events I had consciously ignored, deliberately chosen to file away or pretend never occurred.

Writing my name on the board that day in the woods was like performing an exorcism. I began to think of myself as Mary, not Mildred. But I told no one, so no one knew. They all called me by the name of a person I felt no longer existed. I didn't mind though. I wanted to be the first one to define who Mary was. Life got better, almost immediately. Mum cut off her hair and lost a ton of weight. I suppose she was also redefining herself.

She fell in love with Jonathan, a black American man from Indiana whom she worked with. The color of maplewood, he was a thick mountain of muscles. He had a baby face and bulgy, round veins that webbed the top of his hands. Mum, Paula, and I moved to a townhouse apartment in Silver Spring, down the road from Jonathan's. He came over frequently. I didn't like him at all. I missed my father and even though he rarely called or came to see me, I wanted no replacements. Mum was visibly happier. She smiled a lot, wore nicer clothes, and stopped playing that song. She and I spent less and less time together, and I blamed Jonathan for that. He was always there with us, around us, between us.

By this time, I had completed grade school and was about to enter junior high. Seventh-grade orientation was facilitated by a cute eighth-grade boy named David Hatcher. As soon as I saw David, I tripped sloppily in love. He was lanky and had poor posture, but I loved him anyway. He welcomed me to the session, which was led with a round-table of introductions.

"How 'bout if we go clockwise and start with everyone saying their name along with an adjective beginning with the same letter. A word which describes you. That way we will learn more about you. I'm Daring David."

Everyone came up with such clever adjectives to describe themselves. There was Pinky Pam, Angelic Arleeta, and Funky Frank. My turn came too fast. I said the first thing that stumbled out of my mouth.

"I'm Moody Mary," I blurted, regretting it right away. I saw what I assumed was a look of shock in David's eyes.

"Moody Mary," he repeated. "It's, er . . . Hi. Welcome to Takoma Park Junior High."

On to the next person. The name Mary only stuck for a few weeks. The teachers wouldn't call me that without a note from my mother verifying the change. The kids that had come from my previous school knew me as Mildred, and that is what they insisted on calling me, against my wishes. Even the new students who had initially called me Mary began addressing me as Mildred. I paid them no mind. They could call me whatever they wanted. Everything about me was Mary now.

My birthday coincided with the beginning of the school year; an appropriate day, I figured, to get my first kiss. I waited for David by his locker after the last class period in the sexiest pose I could strike. My arms were folded and my glasses propped high on the flat, nearly nonexistent bridge of my nose.

"It's my birthday today," I announced proudly. David opened his locker and stacked his books neatly inside.

"How nice."

"That's it? How nice?"

"Well, what else am I supposed to say? Happy Birthday! Anything else?"

I stepped closer to him. I felt no apprehension, no shame.

"Yes, a kiss."

David was speechless. He closed his locker, stared at the ground for a moment as if thinking of the proper way to respond, then he turned and hurried down the hall. I followed him around the corner, down the next hallway, and around the next corner. I was ready to follow him wherever, even home. I wanted that kiss. I loved him and was more than prepared to make him love me back.

"What'll it take to make you leave me alone?"

David was exhausted. The whites of his eyes were huge and bright. They were flags of surrender with my dark, circular image chiseled deeply into their centers.

"A kiss."

"A hug," he reasoned.

I agreed to the compromise.

"Okay, a hug."

He stared at me for the briefest of moments, knowing

that I would not leave him alone until I got my hug. We embraced. His grip was weak and perfunctory. Mine was full, tight, needy—all the things I knew love to be.

I missed my father desperately. I hadn't seen much of him since he left. Why didn't he call more often? Didn't he care about me? Slowly, I began to hate him. If he didn't care about me then why should I care for him? Reluctantly, I folded my longing for him like a handkerchief and tucked it away; there wouldn't be any more tears. I pretended that Uncle Paul, my mother's older half-brother, was my father. Uncle Paul was a childless, middle-aged man from London. His accent, which was stiff and proper, complemented his refined manner.

"Mildred, dah-ling," he would say when he came to pick me up for our regular Sunday outings. "Stand up straight. Don't slouch. It is quite unbecoming."

He always greeted me this way.

"My dear," he often told me, "you must learn to be a lady."

Outside of my grandmother, I could think of no one whom I loved more than Uncle Paul. He lived in Washington, D.C., with his long-time companion, Uncle Peter. Uncle Paul was a famous British film actor in his younger years. When his most noted film, *A Taste of Honey*, was featured on the classic movie channel, Mum always let me stay up late to watch it. I was so proud of Uncle Paul I taped his old fan photos on my wall. For years, I emulated him.

He was an important man who knew many important

people. In his home, I heard names like Nina Simone, Roberta Flack; I shared the company of people like Maya Angelou and Frederick Wilkerson. Uncle Paul and Uncle Peter traveled frequently. They sent me postcards and pictures from amazing and faraway places. Because he and my mother shared the same last name, I often lied and told people that he was my father.

"My dad's in Southeast Asia this month," I'd tell my friends, whipping out Uncle Paul's latest postcard as proof. He was what I imagined the perfect father would be. Mum, Paula, and I spent each Christmas with him and Uncle Peter, eating pheasant and trifle. Every year he gave me the same present, a humongous jar filled with money—quarters, dimes, pennies, and an assortment of coins and paper dollars from foreign lands.

"Hurry along upstairs and count your loot," he'd say.

When he was in town, Uncle Paul made time to be with me. We had regular weekend dates for trips to the opera, the ballet, the theatre, or to Gifford's Ice Cream Shop, where we ordered thick, rich vanilla milkshakes. Just before we moved into our apartment in Silver Spring, my grandmother came from Ghana and lived with us for a while. Her name was Comfort, but we called her Auntie C. Having her and Uncle Paul around made all the difference.

Like Mum, Auntie C was extremely picky but I welcomed her nagging because it was always followed with silliness and smiles. She was quite a character, and I was her sidekick, her buddy.

"Oh, Nana-Ama," she would say when she found me watching TV instead of tending to my chores. "Why haven't you washed the dishes? And you need to clean your room. Your Mum's going to be home soon."

"I will," I'd tell her, "but this show is so interesting."
Auntie C would walk into the room, stand in front of the
television set, and hold the power knob. Instead of turning
it off, she would increase the volume, sit next to me, and let
me lean my head on her shoulder as we finished watching
the program. She and I cooked side by side, wrote letters
to relatives in Ghana, watched soap operas together. We
would take the number 17 Ride-On bus to the Langley Park
Shopping Center where she would buy shoes and earrings
and all types of fancy electronic equipment to take back
to Ghana with her. When Mum wasn't around, she would
let me in on family secrets. Nothing scandalous, just stories about Mum's youthful shenanigans or about her own
adventures raising six children.

Because he was such a fixture in our home, Jonathan
and I eventually began to get along. I wasn't as threatened
by his relationship with my mother. Once I started making
an attempt to get to know him, I realized he wasn't all that
bad. He listened to my endless chatter about David. Auntie
C refused to hear anymore about David. When I brought his
name up, she would suck her teeth and roll her eyes.

"Mark my words. Boys that age are nothing but rogues
and ruffians." That said, the subject was closed.

Jonathan sometimes helped me with my homework.
When everybody else was too busy, he watched me practice
my routines for cheerleading try-outs. On the night before
the try-outs he even remembered to wish me luck.

Sunday mornings were peaceful times in our home. I woke
up every Sunday morning to the smell of pancakes and the

oohs, aahs, and Amens of the Southern California Community Choir accompanying Aretha Franklin singing "Mary, Don't You Weep." Through the gentle influence of Beth, my best sixth-grade friend, I started attending a Christian Science church. Mum worked as a pharmacist technician so my house was a stomping ground for doctors, pharmacists, and all kinds of medicinal paraphernalia. Ironically, I despised doctors and rarely took any medicine. For the most part, my family was supportive of my quest for religion. There were worse things I could be doing with my time.

Beth's family picked me up on their way to church. I would stand on the main intersection near my home, dressed in jeans and sneakers, holding the Bible that Auntie C had given to me as a gift. Beth and I attended Sunday School class while the rest of her family, the adults, went to the regular service. After Sunday School Beth and I joined her family in the main room and sang hymns.

The entire congregation was kind to me but when they stood to sing, I felt as if I were in the midst of a funeral. The sound of the organ was mournful; the intonations of the songs were dry and straightforward, nothing at all like the music my mother played at home. Four other black people belonged to the church. They were all part of the same family. When we sang, I couldn't help but to look over at them and wonder if they spent their Sunday mornings like I did, listening to the soul clapping spirituals of black folk before going to church and standing in the blandness of these other people praising the wonders of God and Christ, as Scientist.

As the result of a few positive exchanges and phone conversations, David and I eased into a friendship. We sought each other out in school and spent most of our free time together. The day after I found out I had made the cheerleading squad, David and I walked home together. He lived closer to the school than I did. As we approached his block, we slowed down and held hands.

"You know, I really like you a lot," David said, muddling the tail end of his sentence. This time, it was I who was speechless. The very thing I had been wishing for was actually happening. David and I stood still for a while, then we inched our way toward each other until, at last, our lips met. Finally, the kiss. It would be our first and our last. The romance with David was short-lived, lasting two weeks, at best.

By the time I was mid-way through eighth grade, Auntie C returned to Ghana. Losing her in my life was as devastating as losing my father, maybe even more. I put all my efforts into school activities. In addition to being a cheerleader, I was a member of the track team, the debate team, and the drama club. David, who had become my best friend, was the president of the student government association. We shared everything, usually in notes that we slipped to each other between classes.

David began courting the most popular girl in school, Kiki Franklin, who had big bouncy breasts, long crinkly hair, and funny colored eyes. I had an eye for Wayne Beckford, the sleuth-footed Jamaican boy who lived across the street. He was what Auntie C would call a true hooligan, an ambitionless high school graduate with few worries and many girlfriends. Wayne knew I liked him. How could he not have? I lost all composure when I was around him, but he never gave me a second look.

Some days after school the kids in my neighborhood played touch football on a nearby lawn. One time Wayne joined us for a game. Being so close to him made me nervous. I tripped over my feet and fell hands first into a pile of mud. Wayne was standing right next to me. He traced the seam of the ball with his fingertips before tossing it back on the ground, signaling the end of the game, then he helped me up.

"You can come upstairs to my place to wash off."

His voice was deep yet it bounced lightly across the air. My apartment was no further away than his but I knew that if I didn't go with him then, there might never be a second chance.

He lived in a three-bedroom apartment with his mother, an older sister, and a younger brother. None of them were home. His living room was crowded with couches, a loud mismatch of plaid cushions stuffed inside torn plastic covers. In the bathroom, I washed my face and hands, dutifully removing the dirt from underneath all ten fingernails. When I came out, Wayne had disappeared.

"Wayne," I called, tip-toeing around the clutter.

"Come in here," he replied.

I followed the voice into the bedroom that Wayne shared with his brother. He held out a glass of lemonade that he had poured for me in my absence. In his other hand was a beer. I smiled a slight thank you and took the lemonade. I was tense. My recently washed palms were sticky and itching. Setting his beer down on the black lacquer nightstand, Wayne approached me. We were standing so close I was scared to breathe.

"You so pretty. So so pretty. Look at that face. How'd you get so fine?"

I was stunned, elated. Ugly had been the most common adjective my peers used to describe me. If Wayne never spoke another word to me, that would have been enough. My happiness would have lasted forever.

"Thanks," I managed, taking a sip of the drink.

He extended one arm against my back. With the other, he scooped me up off the ground and carried me to his bed. After he sat me down, he began kissing me, licking the lemonade from the edges of my mouth. I had never been kissed like that before. It was all so romantic. Imitating his motions, following his leads, I kissed him back. My eyes were closed so tightly the insides of my lids looked as if they were on fire. I sat still and enjoyed the warm, fast strokes on my lips and face. This is how I stayed while he unbuttoned my blouse, found the small lumps of flesh on my chest, and sucked them like a hungry infant.

Waves of guilt-filled pleasure went through my heart and crashed against my ribs. They rolled into my stomach and flowed down and around the curve of my pelvis. Down, down, till they escaped from my body. The sudden wetness in my underwear alarmed me. What was it that came gushing out? I was embarrassed, horrified.

"I-I-I have to g-go home n-n-now," I stammered.

"C'mon, don't leave. Don't be a baby. You're too big

for that. You're too pretty for that," Wayne whimpered in between kisses. "We don't have to do anything you don't want to. I promise."

I didn't want to leave but I also didn't want to continue doing what we were doing. I wanted Wayne to stop but I didn't want to make him angry. I desperately wanted him to like me. I stayed and said nothing as he continued to kiss me, nothing when he laid me down on the bed; not even when he took off my pants. Nothing at all.

Eyes closed, I thought of other things besides his tongue, his fingers, and the thick, mysterious liquid making its way down and around my thighs. There was the science project that Jonathan promised to help me put together. "B's" were the lowest grade I could bring home without being chastised. Then there was a sharp pain, a deep, stabbing jolt that made me unleash a murderous scream. My eyes, which were sealed shut, began to water.

"You're just tight. Too tight. I'm not all the way in yet," Wayne mumbled.

He pushed and pulled; I cowered and cried. The last heave brought him fully into me. The pain did not stop. Wayne roamed the landscape of my most private terrain wildly, impulsively, as if it were his, until suddenly he shook, shivered, and collapsed on top of me. The pressure of his torso was unbearable. I writhed and pushed passively against him until he sprung up, a new man, no longer passionate, no longer possessed. He said nothing. What was there to say? He sat upright in his bed sipping his beer, distantly watching me as I fumbled, buttoned, laced, and left.

A gnawing numbness settled into my walk. I was positive that Mum would know what I had just done, that everyone would be able to tell. Bracing myself, I opened the front door of our home. To my surprise and relief, the place was empty. I laid down on my bed in a fetal position, trying to get a grip on my feelings. I had just had sex.

The fact that I hadn't wanted to go all the way with Wayne seemed insignificant. He didn't make me go to his place, nor did he force me to do anything. I felt violated but I told myself I had no right to. I had given Wayne my virginity without the least bit of resistance. I was so ashamed I didn't tell anyone about it, not even David. The illusion of time is that it heals all wounds but the ones that have not been attended to only fester. Days and weeks passed. I grew detached from my body. The world was present, yet distant somehow, gradually pulling itself out of my focus.

One afternoon while Mum was working, Jonathan watched over Paula and me. We were in his apartment. Paula was napping on his bed. Jonathan and I were out in the living room small-talking while he folded his laundry. There was a school basketball game later that evening so I was decked out in my cheerleading outfit—a navy blue sweater and a wide-pleated blue and white miniskirt. I removed my saddle shoes and sat cross-legged on the floor. In the last year, I had grown rather fond of Jonathan. He was somewhere between being a relative, an authority figure, and a friend. In him I found an adult with whom I could talk easily without risk of judgment or punishment. Furthermore, he was an adult who remembered his youth.

"Bet a whole lot of knuckle-head boys are chasing after you. Cheerleaders were always the hottest girls in school," he teased.

"Sort of but not really. They're all stupid."

"You're probably just too damn precocious for them."

"What does preco—What does that mean?"

"Precocious," he repeated, carefully enunciating each syllable. "It means grown, advanced. You're probably too womanish for those young punks."

The accusation of being an advanced or grown woman made me edgy. I thought that maybe he could tell I was no longer a virgin. But how?

"Jonathan, can people tell by just looking if someone is having sex?"

He dropped the undershirt he was folding back into the basket.

"Why?" he asked suspiciously.

Who but a precocious thirteen-year-old would think to outwit a thirty-year-old man?

"Well, one of my girlfriends at school had sex and she thought that maybe, well, she has a gap between her legs now and, uh, well, she just wanted to know so she asked me."

"Why did she think you would know?"

The way he was responding to my questions with his own told me that he was on to me. There was no way to get out of the corner into which I had backed myself; I cut my losses and told him. Everything. What was the worst thing he could do? I knew that he wouldn't tell my mother. Jonathan was cool like that. He had covered for me once or twice before when I needed an alibi.

I began by telling him about the neighborhood football game, my muddy hands, Wayne's invitation to go wash them at his house. I told Jonathan about the lemonade, about Wayne's tongue, how good it all felt at first. I described the way the waves felt as they rushed through my body, the humiliation that drifted through me, the pain. I gave him every feeling, every detail, until there was nothing left to tell.

Abandoning the laundry, Jonathan knelt beside me, took me in his arms. There, I felt secure enough to cry.

"You know," he consoled, "sex isn't always like that. Sometimes sex feels wonderful, but it's supposed to be with someone you love and who loves you. Understand?"

I nodded. There was no need to tell him that I had loved Wayne; I had loved everything about him. The way he called me pretty, the way he held me, kissed me, made me think he loved me too. I sensed that Jonathan understood. I wondered whether my father would have understood me the way Jonathan did, whether we would have ever sat together in the candor of a Saturday afternoon folding laundry and talking so openly. I wanted that from him. I wanted my father. The tears fell harder against my skin.

"It's okay. Shhh . . . it's okay." Jonathan rocked and rocked. "It's okay, Mildred. Your mother doesn't have to know about this. Shhh . . . I love you. You know that. It's okay."

The designs on his sweater felt soft and fuzzy next to my cheek. We swayed in silence. Speech was unnecessary so we just swayed and swayed. He raised my chin with his index finger, lowered his head to mine. The thick pads of his mouth parted to form a peculiar smile. Had I truly been grown, truly been a woman, I would have immediately recognized this as the wily smirk of an animal who had come upon his prey. But I was not grown, not a woman, so when he placed his lips on mine I recognized only the rising motion of waves within me.

What kind of a man uses his erect penis, like the pointed, glistening tip of a blade, to butcher the trust of a child? Hindsight affords us the luxury of entertaining the myths of our myriad possibilities, what we could have or should have done but did not. What kind of a child allows this to happen? It was never his fault, always mine. Couldn't I have run? Couldn't I have screamed? Couldn't I have done anything other than shut my eyes and heed the advice of the thunderous music in my brain, telling me, *Mary, don't you weep?* These questions tortured me in my teens. They turned me to stone under the many male bodies that would later benefit from my adolescent promiscuity.

Self-reflection is necessary for personal growth. As I had hoped, my visit to Takoma Park brought me closer to the roots of my depression. But no traumatic memories surfaced that had not already seeped through my flesh in the sweat of a hard night's sleep. Healing is about much more than remembering. Healing is about reinterpreting events, aligning the fiction with the fact. I had created so many lies to erase my misfortunes and my mistakes. The biggest and most damaging of which were my silences.

———◆———

THE SUMMER BEFORE ninth grade, I tried to kill myself by swallowing some pills. Not a lot, not even enough to cause minor damage. My attempt at suicide was a rather austere means to a much-desired end. Because of the abuse, I was already in the process of dying. I was fading into the pastels of walls, the blues and greens of the outside world. I wanted someone else to notice this, to help me reverse what was happening. I thought if my family and friends knew that I was miserable enough to want to die, they would rush to my aid with love and attention. I thought that things would change. And they did. They got worse.

My mother responded to my suicide attempt with "tough love": I was chastised and placed on punishment. She never knew what the real source of my troubled behavior was because I never told her. I didn't tell anyone. Uncle Paul was always off on some business trip. We rarely went on our Sunday outings anymore. My dad had started calling and coming by to see me, but I had built up so much hostility toward him that none of his efforts made much of an impression on me. The way I saw it, all of the adults in my life were either physically or emotionally unavailable. All except Jonathan.

Mary, the spunky, affable persona I had created, went away in pieces. As did my laughter, my assertiveness, my ability to socialize and to study. I stopped going to church; I stopped participating in school. I began sleeping an average of twelve to fourteen hours a day, no matter how early or how late I went to bed. It was a sumptuous, dreamless sleep, which left me feeling drowsy and inexplicably tired. My habitual oversleeping and sudden lack of interest in school caused my grades to fall. I went from being an extrovert to being a loner. I wanted to get away from everything and everyone near me. And as luck would have it, I was able to.

In the fall of 1981, I went away to attend high school at Foxcroft, an all-girls' boarding school in Middleburg, Virginia. The school was in fox country, perched high atop the rolling hills, not far from the Blue Ridge Mountains. Never had I seen anything so spectacular since I emigrated to America. Acres and acres of beautiful land. Lisa Washington, a friend from Takoma Park Junior High, was also an incoming student at Foxcroft.

On the day of our arrival, Lisa and I carried our luggage to Applegate, the freshman dorm, and paced the hallways together in search of our rooms. There was a note with my name on it taped to the door of the room I was to be living in. The names of my two roommates were also on the note— Polly and Molly.

"Listen to this, Lisa," I said as I read the note aloud. "Polly, Molly, and Mary. Polly and Molly? You've got to be kidding."

"Look on the bright side," Lisa said. "They put Mary on the card, not Mildred."

I had requested that the school use Mary, not Mildred, on all my papers. And, unlike junior high school, they didn't ask for parental approval.

"I know, but Polly and Molly? What the hell kind of names are those?"

Lisa pulled out her copy of the *Preppy Handbook* and held it up for me to see.

"Toto," she said, "I think we're not in Kansas anymore."

Indeed we weren't. Out of the thirty freshmen, there were two other black students—Lisa and a girl from Cleveland named Stephanie. In total, there were eight black girls in a student body of two hundred and nine. There were many foreign students, some of whom actually still lived abroad. The rest of the students were white girls—with surnames like Chesire, Vanderbilt, Dunning, and Bedford—who had credit cards, bank accounts, and real pearls in their jewelry boxes.

Foxcroft was a cross between a finishing school and a military academy, a country club and a prison. The underclassmen slept not in their rooms but on sleeping porches, lined with beds, as if in an orphanage. I refused to sleep there. Each night after lights out was called and the whip (student overseer) had strolled down the hallway to make sure everyone was in bed, I rolled myself up in my comforter, snuck into my room, spread a blanket over the carpet, and fell asleep.

In spite of my initial discomfort, I felt at home at Foxcroft. I liked the girls and made friends quickly. Boarding school offered me many blessings, the most important being the space and the freedom needed to search for personal peace. Gail Wronsky, my freshman year English teacher, was an instrumental guide in that search. She was an eccentric poet—thin, blond, giggly. She was also one of the youngest faculty members.

Ms. Wronsky treated her students as if we were her friends; she made us believe that our overall well-being meant just as much as our education. Her classes were often held in the garden. She would sit barefoot on the grass and read revolutionary, avant-garde poetry to us. Or she would invite us to her off-campus cottage on weekends for tea, discussions of love, war, women's rights, and other topics she wanted us to investigate in our writing assignments. Until Ms. Wronsky, I was not familiar with adult fiction or contemporary poetry. The most provocative books I had ever read were by Judy Blume: *Forever* and *Are You There God? It's Me, Margaret*.

While other teachers beseeched us to learn as much as we possibly could about Descartes and Constantinople, Ms. Wronsky hijacked our hearts with the works of Adrienne Rich, Ntozake Shange, Audre Lorde, Anne Sexton, and Alta. Ms. Wronsky was a radical writer and she challenged us to find our individual voices, to consider our thoughts as sacred.

Writing opened a door that I never knew existed. Most of the poems I wrote then were confessional; they were reconstructions of my spirit, my body—on those pages, I gave birth to myself. Each consonant was a bone, solid as rock. Each vowel was tissue. Each line a vein. Meter and rhyme were rivulets of blood thrashing and throbbing. The spaces between the stanzas were breaths suspended, released.

I found that through poetry I could combine events, facts, and reactions—events that happened to me, reactions that belonged to me—to authenticate my experiences and to relay them to others in an acceptable manner. I learned that people trusted words that were written more than they trusted words that were spoken. In art, my words, my feelings, were suddenly credible.

David remained an integral part of my life. He was also enrolled in a boarding school in Virginia, Episcopal High, one of Foxcroft's unofficial "brother" schools. We saw each other at school mixers and tea parties, but mostly we kept in touch through letters. On his envelopes and in his letters, David would always circle the "D" in his first name with straight lines so it resembled the sun. Underneath both his signature and return address he would write *Here comes the sun*. From the time of my suicide attempt, David had been trying to convince me that better days were ahead. After a few months at Foxcroft, I really started to believe that. I was light years away from the "Moody Mary" he met at the junior high orientation. The suffering was almost gone.

When my parents divorced, my mother added her maiden name to ours. My surname became "Danquah-Brobby." During my freshman year in high school, I dropped the name "Brobby" and began to rethink the name "Mary." Taking a blank piece of paper one evening, I wrote the name "Mary" continuously. It was a rather bland name, but I didn't hate it like I hated Mildred. I didn't want to be bland and anonymous anymore. I wanted to be myself—whatever that was. I toyed with the name, exchanging letters here and there, until I arrived at Meri. When I looked at the name *Meri Danquah* something inside clicked. I felt as if I already owned it. Meri Danquah was not who I would become or pretend to be; it wasn't a persona. It was me, who I had been all along.

When I returned to Foxcroft for my sophomore year, Gail Wronsky was no longer there. The teacher who took her place was a young, quirky African American woman. She too had a passion for poetry and encouraged my writing. I liked her a lot and chose her to be my faculty adviser, but I wasn't able to duplicate the bond I had shared with Ms. Wronsky. When winter set in my moods became erratic. I arranged my class schedule in such a way that I didn't have to get up and be alert so early in the day.

"Morning meeting" was the one thing that stood in the way of my being able to sleep until noon. At eight o'clock every weekday morning, the faculty and student body assembled in the library for roll call and announcements. I would often sleep right though these meetings or show up late, in my nightgown, with uncombed hair and unbrushed teeth. I was grumpy, cantankerous, withdrawn; I felt tired, sad, drained of energy. I got sick frequently. Day after day I trudged across the sprawling campus, through the snow, to the infirmary hoping the

nurse would offer me a place to heal or, at least, hiber-
nate. Day after day the nurse examined me and said that
she could find no indications of any physical health
problems.

The poems I wrote were no longer personal testimonies
of strength and survival. They were dreary and pessimistic:

"Juxtaposition (Time)"

I.

i have been sick
for months now
with a disease
called time
too much time to do nothing
and not enough time to do everything
except parallel the situations
of time

2.

now and then
when i sit adjacent
to the solutions
i attempt (in my own slow manner)
to one by one, deface them

to uncover the falseness
or maybe find a cure
for the nonchalance
which has overcome me
i suppose i should give it time

3.

the questions
though disposed of ages ago
come back every so often
like a boomerang of realization
having pushed one step beyond
the edge of death
or as some say, insanity
i know now that it is time
to leave

Now when I read the poems that I wrote back then, it is obvious to me that I was suffering from depression. I find it rather ironic that in the poem "Juxtaposition" I chose to use the word *disease* to describe the way I was feeling; to indicate that I was in search of a cure.

For financial reasons, I didn't return to Foxcroft after my sophomore year. My junior and senior years were spent at the local public school, Montgomery Blair. While I had been at Foxcroft, Uncle Paul and Uncle Peter moved to Morocco. Other than their absence, my return was like a travel backwards in time. Everything was the same. The majority of the students at Montgomery Blair were people I had gone to elementary and junior high with, people who knew me and still saw me as Mildred.

The feelings of depression that I had experienced at Foxcroft lingered. On December 11, 1983, three months into my junior year, something happened that pushed me deeper into the despair. My neighbor, Jennifer, and I were walking to school. When we reached the first entrance of the school at the boys' gym, Manda, another neighbor, shouted for us to "wait up," so she could walk the rest of the way with us. Jennifer and I stood at the bottom of the steps in front of the gym.

I noticed a student standing on the other side of the street, waiting for the traffic to slow down so she could cross. She glanced left, then right and took a step into the street. She was not even halfway across the first lane when a school bus came speeding around the curve and hit her. Her body was thrown several feet. Her head hit the asphalt. The sounds; those sounds. Wheels skidding, rubber burning, bones cracking. Time stopped. Everything was in slow motion. The bus swerved to avoid hitting her again. But it did. The tires rolled over her legs. I watched them shake as if in a state of seizure.

Somehow Jennifer and I managed to run into the gym and tell the teachers to call 911. When we went back outside, someone was giving the girl mouth to mouth. A crowd had gathered. Inside the bus, there were young children, kindergarten age. The bus driver ran across the street and cornered Jennifer and me. She was hysterical, in tears. A woman who was obviously the young girl's mother was standing over the body wailing. Her shrieks were high pitched. She sounded like an animal being tortured. I looked at the girl's body, her jeans ripped to shreds, the blood on the black road. I looked at her face and realized I knew her. She was Michele, the girl who sat behind me in typing class.

Michele died at the hospital a few days later. She was the first person I had ever known who died. In a strange way, I felt responsible for her death. I felt like it should have been me. Each time I closed my eyes, I saw the bus swinging around the bend; I saw Michele's body hitting the ground over and over. She was an athlete, a top student, a model daughter. But in the end, none of that mattered. It wasn't enough to save her. That just didn't make any sense to me. How could someone like Michele die while people like me kept living?

The school provided professional counseling for those of us who had witnessed the accident. The counselor told me that I shouldn't spend too much time trying to sort out the reasons why Michele had died; it was simply her time. That got me to wondering when my time would come. It was as if I suddenly realized that I was not invincible, that even though I was young, I could die at any second. This hurled me into a wicked desire to live. Not so much to stop and smell the roses but to push the boundaries of my existence, to test fate. I became reckless.

I started having sex with Roberto, a boy I had been dating. He was a student at Fork Union Military Academy in Virginia who was home for Christmas. It was the first time I had been with someone of my own choosing. Roberto was gentle and loving, but it made no difference. My body was limp and unresponsive. Wayne and Jonathan floated through my thoughts. Roberto pushed, pumped, pulled. I lay still with my breath held at the base of my diaphragm. He was in ecstasy; I was in agony. I got pregnant and had an abortion. It was only a month and a half after Michele's death.

Roberto called me when he returned home for Spring Break. We made plans to meet at the McDonald's in downtown Silver Spring. I waited ten minutes for the bus. When it didn't come, I decided to walk. I stopped at the intersection where Michele had been killed and sat on the steps in front of the gym. In the distance, I could almost hear the howling sound Michele's mother let out when she saw her daughter lying on the asphalt. I placed my hands on my empty womb and started crying.

I didn't want to see Roberto. Not when I knew he'd be leaving again in two weeks. I couldn't bear to lose the presence of one more person in my life. What I wanted was for someone to hold me, to love me, and to stay forever. But I knew that would never happen. In my life, love was synonymous with loss. Love was fleeting. It was a feeble promise in an unsteady world. I got up, walked back to the apartment and went to sleep. Roberto and I never saw each other again.

After the abortion, my mother and I fought all the time. There was nothing I could do to win her praise. She thought I was completely out of control, a hopeless case. I was lazy, my grades were bad, all of my friends—except David—were juvenile delinquents. Whenever David called from school and she answered the phone, she bent his ear for long periods of time telling him how much of a degenerate I was; that I was stupid, a failure, a loser, a slut. The first three or four times this happened, David took it in stride. "I'm really sorry you feel this way," he'd tell her. When he finally got tired of having to go through this, he started calling when he knew she would not be home.

Senior year rushed by me with lightning speed. In September of that year, 1984, my father remarried. I started spending every other weekend at his house. Being there was like heaven. We were making good progress in our relationship. His new wife, Anne, was ten years older than me. She didn't try to assume a maternal role in my life. I saw her more as an older sister or cousin, not a parent. Like me, Anne loved literature. We would sit and talk for hours about books and movies and current events. I allowed myself to get close to her and I began to trust the fact that my father was back in my life for good.

The developing friendship that my stepmother and I shared was a sore point between me and my mother. After my visits with my father and stepmother, Mum would go into a tirade. She reminded me that after Daddy left, it was she who had struggled and sacrificed everything to raise us. It was clear that by befriending Anne, I was betraying my mother. And despite the fact that Mum and I were going through a difficult time, I did not want her to feel betrayed by me. I knew the pain she had gone through after the divorce. I saw how hard she worked to make ends meet in our home.

It was a difficult position for me to be in. But, ultimately, one that I felt was easily remediable by placing distance between myself and my father. He had, after all, abandoned us. I owed him no allegiance. If he had only stayed, life would be so different for all of us. When he called, I was mean, nasty, and rude to him. When he finally stopped calling, I was sick with pain. I went back and forth like this, between rage and regret, until my emotions completely shut down.

At school, a group of girls and I formed a clique that we called The Hallway Crew. We met in the hallway every day after homeroom and ditched school. Some days we drove to the 7-Eleven at the Takoma Metro Station and bought beer. By nine o'clock in the morning, we were at someone's house, drunk out of our minds. Sex and alcohol went hand in hand. There were days when I would wake up in the afternoon lying on a strange bed, naked, smelling of sex, but unable to recall what I had done and who I had done it with. My actions were motivated by pure disconsolateness.

Sex meant everything and, at the same time, nothing to me. It meant being held, being wanted. It was a safe place for tears and for reassurance. When I cried, my lovers wiped my eyes; they pulled me closer, softened their voices, and gave me what I believed was the best of themselves.

———◆———

IN JULY OF 1985, a month after I graduated from high school, James Hawkins, a close friend of mine, was killed in a freak motorcycle accident. James and I had known each other since grade school and had recently renewed our friendship. His death hit me harder than Michele's. This time, I was sure that my own tragic demise was out there waiting for me. When I slept, I dreamed of the many ways that death would snare me.

David was home for the summer. He had just completed his first year as a journalism major at Boston University. James's death had a profound effect on David as well. He traded in his khaki pants and Lacoste shirts for black jeans and black tee-shirts. He shaved off all his hair and started saying things like, "It's now or never," and "Tomorrow is not guaranteed." Each weekend David and I would take the Metro to Georgetown where we would sit in a secluded booth at Pizzeria Uno spouting existentialist theories and commiserating over watered down beer about how the world was definitely coming to an end.

David got over his funk before the time came for him to go back to Boston. Midway through his final week at home, we went to the McDonald's in downtown Silver Spring for burgers and fries. It was the last time we would see each other until his next break from school.

"What are you going to do about college?" he asked me.

"I don't know," I replied. "Maybe I'll enroll in cosmetology school."

He had a concerned look on his face. It was the same exact look he gave me for weeks after my suicide attempt.

"You're not really serious, are you?"

"David," I laughed. "It's a joke. I don't know what I'm going to do. I might not even go."

"Sure you will," he said, "and I bet you we'll end up working for the same paper in someplace like Boise, Idaho."

I smiled and fought hard to keep from crying. All through high school, we had each talked about majoring in journalism and writing for a living. He seemed to be on the right track. It didn't take much to see that his life was coming together and that mine was falling apart. I didn't have the same drive for success that I used to. I could barely muster up enough incentive to get up in the mornings.

We finished our meals and left. We walked around the corner to Georgia Avenue, the main boulevard.

"If you decide against cosmetology school, you can always go there," David said pointing at the building next door to McDonald's. It was the Ronald McDonald Hamburger College. We both laughed at his joke until we reached a point of nervous discomfort. Of the goodbyes that he and I had said, this was the most painful. We both knew that when he returned, I would be right there, standing in the same place where he had left me. For the last six years, he had been my best friend. And now, I was losing him, too. I stopped walking and stared at the ground.

"David," I said, "I think we should just say goodbye now."

"Why?" he wanted to know.

I turned and pointed toward where I lived.

"That's where I'm going." I then pointed toward where he lived. "And that's where you're going. They're in entirely different directions."

I spent the next two years dropping in and out of different colleges in the area and working miscellaneous dead-end jobs. In August of 1987, I moved to Southern California. I had an uncle who lived there, and it was the farthest place I could think of. I wanted to do more than move past the imperfections of my history; I wanted to turn my back on everything, everyone, and keep walking till I could see a sun coming over my horizon.

———◆———

LOOKING BACK AT my past, I saw a definite pattern of depression. To the extent that the initial breakdown I had in Los Angeles seemed rather inevitable. Still, I continued to tell myself that these cycles were well within my control, especially since I was now aware of them; I was capable of rising above my tendency toward depression and getting my life back on track. This made me feel happy and hopeful.

On Monday morning, two days after my visit to Takoma Park, I relapsed. I couldn't even get out of bed that morning. I had woken up in the middle of the night and been unable to go back to sleep. Even though I was wide awake, I couldn't move. The longer I lay there, the more difficult it was. My mind was filled with all sorts of negative thoughts. I kept telling myself that I would never amount to anything, that I was fooling myself if I thought I was strong enough to beat the depression. I tried to override these thoughts by feeding myself positive messages. You're doing the best you can as fast as you can, I told myself, over and over.

Then Korama woke up. I was able to pull myself out of my thoughts, and out of bed, to get her off to nursery school on time. Since I had managed to do that, I was certain that getting through the rest of the day would prove to be easier. Mind over matter, I kept repeating on the way home from the nursery school, mind over matter. I reassured myself that meeting my Smithsonian deadline could not possibly be as hard as I was making it out to be.

All I had to do was run into the apartment, grab my purse, notebook, and pen, then run back out. After that, I would go to the archives, make copies of everything that I needed and bring the material back home. At home, I would go over the papers and toss out the ones I didn't need. If I could stick to that routine for the rest of the week, I would be able to show up at the meeting on Friday and make my deadline. When I got inside, I sat on the bed and stared at the wall for hours. Then I laid down and pulled the covers over me. I didn't budge until it was time to get Korama from nursery school.

The next day was worse. I wasn't able to pull myself together to take Korama to nursery school before the cut-off time. I turned the television on to PBS and let her sit next to me in bed while she watched *Sesame Street*. I wasn't asleep, but I might as well have been. Korama sat there sucking her thumb. Ernie, Bert, and Big Bird were not holding her attention. She was hungry. Each time she turned and looked at me, a pang of guilt stabbed through my chest. Her eyes were dismal and droopy. I forced myself out of bed and made her breakfast.

When she finished picking at her food, she climbed into the bed, and placed her head on my stomach. My heart was breaking for her. Inside of me there was a vibrant, eager mother who wanted to take her daughter to the park and play. There was a reliable, hard-working woman who wanted to fulfill the requirements of her employment contract. If only I could just find a way to get past this impediment.

I called Scott and begged him to come over. I told him I had a stomach virus and was too sick to tend to Korama. Before he got there, I washed Korama up, brushed her teeth, combed her hair, and threw some day clothes on her. I didn't bother to do the same for myself. I was wearing the clothes that I had slept in, the same ones I had worn the day before. Scott sat with us for a few hours. I stayed in bed and listened to him read book after book to Korama. They counted fingers together, played with her toys, and chatted up a storm.

Scott coaxed me into leaving the house and walking his dogs with him. When we returned to his house from the walk, he volunteered to make Korama and me dinner. I didn't have much of an appetite, but he and Korama ate enough for the three of us. After dinner, Scott walked us back to my apartment and volunteered to put Korama to bed for me.

"Are you going to be alright?" he wanted to know.

"Yes," I said, hoping it was the truth.

"Please call if you need me to come watch the baby again. I really don't mind. Feel better."

I didn't fall asleep until four o'clock in the morning. I took Scott up on his offer and asked him to come over the next day as well. I was doing a little bit better than the day before. Korama had been bathed, dressed, and fed by the time Scott showed up.

"Still not feeling well?" he asked when he walked in.

I nodded. I noticed that he was staring at me strangely.

"What's wrong?"

"Oh nothing. Just admiring your sweater."

It was my old maternity sweater, a black and white swirl of thick yarn with big, silky pink bows around the collar. When I realized that I was wearing the same clothes he had seen me in the day before and the day before that, I excused myself and took my first shower in two days. The next day, I woke up early and was able to get going without much difficulty. Korama got off to school alright and I made it through the whole day without having to take to my bed.

On Friday, an hour before my appointment at the Smithsonian, I called to cancel. I told them that I couldn't make the meeting because I was sick, but that I would drop the material in the mail. The project coordinator sounded disgusted. How many meetings had I canceled? How many excuses had she heard? I felt like a louse. I wanted to find a way to let her know that I was not a flake or a fraud. I wished that she could have been able to see me when I was at my best, when I was a considerate, aggressive woman, fully capable of achieving anything I set my mind to.

In the years that followed, I would feel like this many times, like if people only understood what was really going on, they would be more sympathetic. These feelings were quickly obliterated by the realization that when it came to depression, there was a shortage of understanding and sympathy. It simply was not looked upon as a legitimate illness. Most employers really don't give a damn if you're depressed, and neither do landlords or bill collectors.

More than any of the appointments that I've canceled, friends that I've lost, or projects that I have bungled on account of depression, what I most regret are the times that I was unable to properly tend to my daughter's needs. When I could, I found someone else to take care of her. But many times, that was not possible, so she stayed by my side, trapped in my depression with me.

I was determined to finish the project and drop it in the mail. I called my mother and asked her if Korama could spend the weekend at her place.

"Where are you going to be?" she wanted to know.

"I just need to get through all this work," I said.

"You know I'll always make time for Korama. I won't be home till five-thirty but Paula should be there by three. Why don't you just leave her with Paula so that way you can take the bus back before it stops running."

Scott walked with Korama and me to the subway station near our home and asked that I call him when we got to The Ivy. I could tell that he was worried about me. He had been extremely helpful those last couple of days. If he hadn't been around, I don't know what I would have done. When I got to my mother's, Paula was sitting at the dining room table reading the newspaper. She was holding a pen in her hand.

"You do the crossword in ink?" I asked her.

Korama ran up to her and sat on her lap. Paula put the pen down and wrapped her arms around Korama.

"What'd you say?" she asked.

I stood behind her chair and bent down to give her a kiss on the cheek. My eyes glanced over the newsprint as I lowered my head. She had been reading the obituary page.

"Why are you reading the obituaries? That's really morbid."

"No it's not. I'm just looking to see if anyone I know died."

"You're fifteen years old, Paula. How many people could you possibly know that are dying?"

"Oh, you'd be surprised, Nana-Ama," she said. "After all, D.C. is the murder capital of the nation now. A whole bunch of fifteen-year-old kids are lying in caskets."

She turned and faced me. The last thing I wanted to do was think, talk, or hear about death. I picked up the phone, dialed Jade's number.

"A few days ago this guy I know broke out of juvie. He and his boys jacked somebody and drove the car to Hyattsville. The police caught them breaking into a house. When they busted him, he jumped out of the window and killed himself. It wasn't that much of a surprise to anybody because he had told us all that he would rather die than be locked up again."

There was no answer at Jade's. I looked at my watch. It was four o'clock. The last bus to the subway station was leaving at four-thirty. It would take at least fifteen minutes to walk through the corn fields to get to the bus stop.

"That's horrible, Pooh. How'd you end up being friends with someone like that?"

"We weren't friends. I just knew him. I met him in my advanced English class."

I wanted to stay and talk with her, but if I was going to catch that bus, I had to leave.

"I've gotta go, Pooh. I'm sorry. Can we talk about this later?"

A sad look traveled down her face. She handed Korama to me and returned to her newspaper. I gave Korama a hug goodbye, said thank you to Paula, and left.

When I exited the Metro in D.C. and saw the pay phones on the station platform, I remembered that Scott had asked me to call him. Like everything else I had screwed up recently, my intentions had been good; I had meant to call him. It just slipped my mind.

"The road to hell," I said out loud as I stepped onto the train. "I am on the road to hell."

Back at home, there was a message from Eugene on the answering machine. When we spoke earlier in the week, I told him that I was ready to acknowledge the fact that I suffered from depression. I thought he would be ecstatic to hear that but all he had to say was, "Have you found a therapist?" He didn't seem surprised to hear that I had no desire whatsoever to go into therapy. Ever since that conversation, I had been dodging his calls. I knew that he was going to try to talk me into going to therapy, and I was in no mood to defend the reasons why I refused to.

Back then I was extremely opposed to therapy. I couldn't see myself opening up to a stranger and telling him my most private thoughts. That would feel too weird. It just wasn't a part of the culture I had been brought up with, one in which the public perception of an individual was most important. Now when I think about it, my past aversion to therapy seems irrational. It just boiled down to the simple fact that I didn't want people thinking I was crazy.

Bryan Dunning stopped by on his way home from work. We ended up grabbing a bite to eat at a nearby diner. As he escorted me back to my apartment, an all-too-familiar feeling of loneliness fell over me. I didn't want to go back to my dark apartment and spend the rest of the evening by myself.

"I don't want to go home," I told him. "If you don't have anything else to do, let's catch a movie or go to a club."

"I could go for that," he said, "but I need to stop by my place and get out of this suit."

On the way to Bryan's house, we passed by a brownstone with a lively party going on inside. Bryan and I watched a group of young men walking up to the house. When the front door opened, we could see dozens of people milling around. I tugged at Bryan's shirt. Without a word, he knew what was on my mind. We had crashed many a party together when we were in Los Angeles.

"The suit, Meri," he reminded me. "We can come back after I change. I don't want to stick out."

With or without the suit, Bryan would have naturally blended in with the crowd. As the only black person there, I was the one that stuck out. People kept coming up to me and asking, "Are you a friend of Joe's?" I guessed that Joe was the one throwing the party. Either that or he was another black person I hadn't yet spotted. The party was not as happening as we thought it would be. There was a keg in the back yard so we went outside to grab ourselves some beer. Bryan ran into someone he knew and the two of them went off into a corner to catch up. I positioned myself by the keg and drank cup after cup.

I should have been enjoying myself, but I wasn't. With all those people around me, I felt just as lonely as I would have had I gone home and stayed in bed. I wondered if this was what Jade had felt like that day she was at the arcade. It's like you're there, but not really. Like your life is colliding with someone else's version of reality, but the impact isn't forceful enough to throw you out of your insulated cubicle; like everything going on around you is merely a three-dimensional backdrop to your pain. The surest way I knew to deaden the pain was by self-medicating with alcohol, so I drank up until I couldn't feel a thing.

———◆———

DECEMBER BEGAN LIKE November ended, with the limbs of trees losing their leaves and the winds of ever-changing moods sweeping me away. Korama and I prepared to go to L.A. for a visit. When the court granted me permission to relocate with Korama, they allowed Justin two one-week visitations with her each year; the first of which he was to pay for. In late November, he sent two airplane tickets for us to go to Los Angeles.

The thought of seeing Justin again twisted my stomach into knots. I predicted that during our visit the proverbial "other shoe" would definitely drop. Each night, until the day of our departure, I worried myself into panic attacks. I would dream up the worst possible scenarios and work myself up to a breathless frenzy of fear. It was all I could think about. Whenever I told Eugene about my fear of a violent confrontation between Justin and me, he would laugh and say, "You're tripping, Meri. It ain't that deep. You've been gone for six months. If he was gonna do anything, he'd have done it by now."

As the plane landed on the runway at LAX, my paranoia vanished. When Korama and I arrived at my girlfriend Charlene's apartment, I was so thrilled to be back in Los Angeles, I had all but forgotten about Justin. It was a warm, breezy day and the sun was bright. The city was a sight for sore eyes. I missed it so much; the weather, the landscape, the space. Space between houses, space between the palm trees lining the blocks. The street names were written on large, blue signs with space between the fat, white letters. Space and sunshine. Charlene's apartment was enormous and the light streamed through the windows. How could I have left all this? I wondered; I must have been insane.

I called Justin right away to let him know that we had arrived. He sounded excited about seeing Korama. He gave me a tentative schedule of the times he wanted to pick her up. I hoped that either Charlene or her roommate would be with me whenever he was around. There was no way he would act up in front of other people. It wasn't his style. His public image was too important to him. But the next evening when he came to get Korama, he was fifteen minutes early. Neither Charlene nor her roommate had returned from work.

When I heard the knock at the door, my heart somersaulted into my throat. I was so nervous I could have peed my pants.

"Hi, Nana-Ama," Justin said when I opened the door.

I nodded and smiled, but no words came out. I was amazed at how thin and weak-looking he was. This was the man who had hit me? *This* was the man who had belittled me? The one for whom I had lowered my already low self-esteem? There was no way. He was as nervous about seeing me as I had been about seeing him. I could sense it. Where had all his power gone? I stood in front of him with composure and the supreme knowledge that he could do me absolutely no harm. Eugene was right. It wasn't that deep. I stepped to the side and motioned for Justin to come in. The authority I felt was so delicious, I wanted to belch out a vulgar laugh of freedom and be done with the joke of our history.

While Korama was visiting with her father, I went to the movies, played catch-up with friends. The depression released its hold over me. My relationship with—and to—the world changed; I felt like a participant, not an invisible observer. It was no longer a struggle to get up, to stand up, to walk, to run. I felt alive. Listening to the chirping of the birds in the morning was a delight, not an annoyance. At the end of the week, I didn't want to leave Los Angeles.

The depression did not return when I got back to D.C., but I was unhappy. The city was cold and claustrophobic, not warm and spacious, like L.A. I resented the fact that my apartment received very little sunlight. And I hated the idea of starting over, rebuilding my career. I had worked long and hard in Los Angeles to establish myself as an emerging artist. I knew the ins and outs of the art world. In a pinch, I could always scramble up a good gig for myself. It took me five years to establish that base. I didn't know any arts administrators in D.C. and, after the mess I had made of the Smithsonian contract, it was doubtful that anyone would refer me for anymore contracts or jobs.

With the physical symptoms of the depression gone, I was able to finally complete the Smithsonian project and hand it in. All of the independent contractors who worked on that assignment were given new contracts for another exhibition—except me. It was obvious that the Smithsonian was not going to be needing my services anytime in the near future. I was left with no other choice but to go back to temping. It was a bad time to be looking for a job in D.C. Christmas was just around the corner. And the city was preparing itself to receive the newly elected president. I went ahead and signed up at several employment agencies even though I knew that the chances of getting an assignment were slim to none.

But I didn't waste my time away in bed. I was bursting with energy. So what if I didn't have a 9 to 5? The anthology project was still there. I worked on it night and day. When I wasn't sitting at the computer writing letters to contributors, I was busy with household chores. With the exception of the fact that I had no gainful employment, things were fine. I wonder how long I would have been able to maintain that period of emotional stability if poverty hadn't worn me out.

Too much stress makes it hard to keep the faith. And money, or lack thereof, can be a major source of stress. I got more bills in the mail than Christmas cards and my creditors called more frequently than my friends. Financial worries spilled over into every other aspect of my life. It became hard to focus on anything else. A colleague of mine gave my name to an editor at *The Washington Post* who was looking for someone to write a "poetic" article. I landed the assignment but by then all of my confidence had been sucked up. It was like the Smithsonian project all over again. I just couldn't write the article.

Washington, D.C., had taken as much of a toll on me as I was going to let it. When the New Year rolled around, the one resolution I made was to get out of town. If the depression was going to be inescapable, then why not contend with it in a city that I liked? Why not live where I wanted to?

"You're just going to pack up and go back to L.A.?" my father asked when I told him that I was leaving.

"Yup," I said.

"What if you go back and you decide you don't like it there? What are you going to do? Pack up and come back to D.C.?"

"Yup," I repeated.

"You can't just keep moving back and forth like that, Nana-Ama. You have to settle down."

"Why?"

"Because you're a mother. You have to grow up now. It's

not just you anymore. You can't keep running from place to place. Children need stability."

"Children need love," I snapped back. "My love is stable."

My mother's reaction was pretty much the same as my father's.

"You change your mind like you change your underwear," she announced.

"No I don't. I never said I was going to stay in D.C. forever."

"You haven't even stayed for a year," she continued. "What do you think is going to be in L.A. that wasn't there when you left?"

"It's not about what's changed in L.A., it's about what's changed in my life," I explained. "Korama's older now. I'll be able to manage better."

"Humph. If you say so. Not that you ever listen to me, but I think you're making a big mistake."

"It's my life, Mummy. I'm not happy here. And if I go to L.A. and I'm not happy there, I'll go somewhere else."

"Happy? Nana-Ama, you can't be happy all of the time. Look around you. There are a lot of unhappy people, but they don't keep moving back and forth across the country. Let's not even get into this. You're gonna do whatever you want to do. Your way is the right way. You've always been hard-headed."

The thought of telling my mother about my bouts with depression never crossed my mind. I had never been very communicative or forthcoming with either of my parents about anything. I always did them the great disservice of assuming that they were completely clueless when it came to me, and I wasn't about to expend any energy on bringing them up to speed. Consequently, their advice and admonitions usually fell on deaf ears. When I told them that I was returning to Los Angeles, they immediately saw what my desperation kept me from seeing—that I was trying, once again, to outrun my problems.

My parents were so adamantly opposed to the idea of my leaving Washington I began to have doubts about whether or not I was, indeed, making a mistake. Maybe I was being too rash. I called Eugene to get his opinion. Not that I would have been any more receptive to his opposition than I was to my parents'. My mother was right about one thing, I was hard-headed; I did as I pleased. That had nothing to do with depression. Whereas I chose to leave, another individual in the same situation might have opted to stay. The manner in which depressives respond to the illness has just as much to do with their nondepressed personalities—who they really are—as it does with any other circumstance. Eugene gave me his blessings.

"You should go wherever you're most comfortable," he said. He did, however, caution me to make certain I was moving because I truly wanted to and not because I was searching for an escape.

"Don't go cutting off your nose to spite your face," he warned. "You'll still hate the reflection you see."

Paula didn't take the news well. She kept her eyes on the floor, which was alright with me because I didn't want to see her face. It would be a disappointed face, one that she seemed to be wearing more and more in my presence. It would be the face of a child who had been told time and again to wait and, after patiently waiting, had finally sensed that what she had been wanting and waiting for would never come. I knew that Paula had been hoping for much more from me by way of time and attention. I didn't want her to be disappointed. For me, disappointment was far worse than anger; it was worse even than hate. I wanted her to be mad. I wanted her indignation to alleviate my guilt.

"Tell me what's on your mind," I said. "I know you're probably angry at me. Talk to me. Tell me how you feel."

She said nothing.

"Pooh, are you listening to me?" I asked.

"Uh-huh," was her reply.

"Yell, scream. Say something."

Still nothing.

"You love L.A. You can come visit."

"It's not the same, Nana-Ama," she reminded me, her eyes throwing daggers into mine. "Why do you have to go? You promised that you and Korama . . . You said you were staying. You said you were coming back for good."

I repeated to her what Daddy had said to me a long time ago when I asked him why he was leaving us.

"This is something I have to do. One day you'll understand."

I was eleven years old then. My heart splintered and the tiny fragments shot off, like fireworks, inside my chest. The disappointment was wrenching. It wounded me more than anything ever had. Paula didn't look at me, she didn't move or say a word. She didn't have to.

———

ON THE TWENTY-FIRST of February 1993 I was scheduled to return to L.A. I had used the last of my savings to ship our stuff and pay for the airfare. Scott said he would buy my computer from me. That was all the money I would have to my name when I went back. My father's brother, Reks, had recently moved back to L.A. from Ghana. He said that Korama and I could crash at his apartment for a month or so. The rest, I told myself, would fall in place. It had to.

After weeks of phone tag, I was able to reach Jade. I didn't want to leave without saying goodbye to her.

"Meri," Jade said when she recognized my voice. "I was going to call you."

"Yeah, right," I said under my breath. I hadn't heard from her in weeks. I had called several times and left word. She never returned my calls. It seemed senseless at this point to give her any grief about her disappearing act. "Happy Valentine's Day, Jade."

"Same to you," she muttered. "Like I was saying, I was going to call you because, well, because I wanted to tell you how great it's been knowing you. Aaron was right when he said that we'd hit it off. I've had so much fun hanging out with you. I feel like I've known you all my life. This is going to sound strange coming from me, but I wanted to remind you to give yourself a break sometimes. You are doing so well. Don't let the depression get the best of you. You have to beat this thing. You have to."

The goodbye appeared to be more hers than mine. In fact, it was more like a swan song. A keen and supplicating, yet, ultimately, conclusive melody. She's going to kill herself, I thought.

"Is one of us going somewhere?" I asked her. I was praying she would say that either my mother or Paula had told her I was leaving.

"No. I just wanted to tell you what was on my mind. Life is short, you know. It's good to let people know how you feel."

Her answer confirmed my suspicion. I didn't know what to say, what to do. Over the course of our friendship, Jade had mentioned death several times. We both had. We had talked about wanting to die, not about killing ourselves. I suppose one eventually can lead to the other. I tried to place myself in Jade's shoes. If I were contemplating suicide and someone confronted me about it, I would most likely get defensive and deny it. If I was going to try to extract her confidence, it would have to be done in person.

"You're right," I told her. "Life is short. I feel the same way about you, too. The reason I called is that there's something important I need to tell you. I have to do it face to face, and I have to do it tonight. I'm being taken out for Valentine's Day. Can you join us? We can talk afterwards."

"I'm not going to crash your date," she said.

"Date? I'm going to dinner with Korama and my neighbor, Scott. I would hardly call that a date. Please come. It'll be a free meal."

She refused several times, said she didn't feel like going out. I had to let the cat out of the bag.

"You have to come," I whined. "It's sort of a farewell dinner. Korama and I are moving back to L.A. in a week. So, will you come?"

There was a long pause. That meant she was taking it into consideration, a good sign. I crossed my fingers tight and waited through the silence hoping that when it ended, I would hear the word yes.

By evening's end, Jade and I were back in our usual spot on my living room floor. I had just finished moving Korama's cot into the back room.

"Tonight," Jade admitted, "I was planning on killing myself."

I looked at her. She was wearing a long, flowing skirt. Her make-up was subtle, almost unnoticeable. She was leaning against the mattress, her legs stretched out fully so that the hem of her skirt hung over her toes. Her whole presence was one of comfort. Or so I would have presumed had I not known any better.

"I know," I told her, pretending to be unaffected by her disclosure.

"How did you guess?" she asked.

"Miss Thing," I said, "you are not the only one who can recognize a mask. The one you were wearing was pretty transparent anyway. I mean, c'mon, 'Meri, it's been so nice knowing you.' "

She laughed, and in the most imaginative way I could, I continued to speak with her about her planned suicide as if I understood. But I did not.

My ability to identify with her suffering ended at the thought of her taking her own life. Yes, depression was harsh and insufferable. Yes, it was exasperating to live in a nexus of anguish that was seemingly impervious to everything that would seek to obliterate it. But to kill yourself? Was life not an obligation? I mean, were we not meant to lead the life we were given until it reached its natural end? I knew what it felt like to not want to be alive. That didn't make me any more sympathetic to Jade's desire to kill herself.

"*Why?*" I wanted to ask her. "*Why do you want to kill yourself? Think about it as much as you want, but for God's sake, don't do it.*" Instead, I said, "Jade, I know what you're feeling, but—"

"You don't know," she interrupted.

"Of course I do."

I was primed to offer her an anecdote, to tell her about the pills I had swallowed during high school. She didn't give me the opportunity.

"You know what you feel, you don't know what I feel. If it were you in my position and me in yours, I would tell you not to do it. I wouldn't want to see you die, but it's a different view from the outside looking in. What you're looking at is a figment of your imagination. It isn't really me."

What could I possibly say? She was right. People bank too heavily on outward appearances. They assume that what they see is what you are. But how does one get around doing that? Even though I knew Jade had reached her emotional breaking point, it was hard for me to not buy into the deceptive hopefulness of her appearance. What I saw before me was a woman who was poised, thoughtful, and wise; a woman whom I suspected could accomplish whatever she wanted, if she set her mind to it. It was inconceivable that someone like Jade could want to kill herself.

Suicidal ideation is depression's most common and harmful symptom. While most of us who are suffering from depression only contemplate death, many depressives find themselves in such great pain that they do actually make the attempt at killing themselves. It is difficult for those of us who survive them to understand why they felt death was their last resort. "What can make someone take their own life?" we ask. Depression can. It can make the improbable become possible; it can make death look like a valid option.

It is not easy for everyone to accept suicide as an extreme function of depression. We live in a society that regards suicide as a sin, an act of cowardice, and a basis for shame. In *Searching for Mercy Street*, Linda Gray Sexton explains that "Suicide is an immediate and permanent solution to pain. The pain can be either physical or emotional: an emotional pain of an intensity sufficient to drive the sufferer to consider suicide often manifests itself in physical symptoms so powerful that to quibble about origin is beside the point. Pain is pain regardless of its source. None of these conditions can necessarily be conquered by willpower; neither are they induced by laziness, lack of moral ethic or selfishness."

It was only after Linda Gray Sexton had suffered through her own depression that she was able to finally come to terms with the suicide of her mother, renowned poet, Anne Sexton. "In my mind," she explains, "I had accused my mother of these failings many times. Now, my own experience had taught me a different and quite simple lesson: suicide is a synonym for escape. My mother died of depression."

Part of the reason I was not willing to empathize with Jade's desire to end her life (and, as a result, end her pain) was that it meant I'd have to accept the prospect of once again losing someone dear.

"Jade Parsons," I said, jumping to my feet, "get with the program. Pull yourself together." It was a serious sentiment but I made it sound as if it were a joke.

"By my bootstraps?" she asked, laughing.

"Yes," I said, laughing with her. It tickled me to think that I was resorting to the same silly cliché that people often tell depressives. I thought of all the other homilies that I had heard over the years. "Snap out of it. Tomorrow is another day. Be positive. Think of all the people who love you. Life is a series of ups and downs."

The one thing Jade and I shared was a twisted, impregnable sense of humor. She found my sarcasm quite hilarious.

"No," she added, "life is a bowl of cherries."

Before she could finish the rest of the sentence, we fell out hootin' and hollerin'. Jade stopped laughing and shook her head from side to side.

"Girl," she sighed, "some of the shit people think to say."

We sat in silence for a few minutes. I could tell by the vacant expression on her face that she was lost in her thoughts again.

"What's going through your mind?" I asked.

"I wouldn't know where to begin. You don't even know the half of it, Meri."

"Yes I do. You told me, remember? You told me about being in the arcade with your friend and feeling closed in, you told me about standing on the balcony of your house thinking about jumping."

"Oh yeah," she said. "I did, didn't I? I should have jumped when I was on that balcony that night."

"Why didn't you?" I asked, hoping the question didn't sound too callous.

"I don't know. When I heard that Jordan wouldn't even think about going out with me because I'm black, it was like everything came crashing down at the same time. I guess everything was already coming apart before that and he was just the straw that broke the camel's back."

"Did you feel the same way you do now? Like killing yourself?"

"I felt like dying, but I didn't feel like killing myself. Does that make sense? The thought of jumping just sort of went through my mind real quick, and I leaned over the railing."

"But you got through it," I said, patting her hand, "and everything ended up okay."

"I got through it, but everything wasn't okay. That year, I got kicked out of the gifted and talented program because my grades were so poor. I was spiraling and my parents didn't know how to help me. My father is like a genius or something. He would sit there with me and do math homework, but he would put me down by saying things like, 'You don't know that?' or 'What's wrong with you?' "

"At least you had a father that was there."

"Yeah, he was there alright, but he wasn't supportive. So I just said, 'Fuck it.' That became my general attitude toward everything. I had always been in the special classes, the quote-unquote smart classes, which were always filled with preppy white people. They pulled me out and I ended up in an entirely different environment, classes filled with poor white trash, Hispanics, and blacks—the same black students who had ostracized me throughout the years and called me 'oreo,' 'wannabe,' and stuff."

"That must have been a pretty hard adjustment for you to make."

"Nope. If you can believe it, those kids were the ones that actually ended up saving me. By the time I joined their class, I didn't care anymore, nothing could make me feel any worse than I already did. And I guess they noticed. They started being nice to me and sometimes they would come up to me in the hallway and say, 'Jade, you look so sad.' They proved themselves to be good people, better than those other kids who thought they were all hoity-toity because they had been told they were smart. Being accepted by the other black kids sort of blunted my depression, but it didn't help my grades. I barely made it through the ninth grade."

"Your parents never noticed what was happening?"

"They did, Meri. But by that time, I was far gone. I wouldn't go to school. I would wake up every morning and freak out. I couldn't leave the house. I would leave my house and have panic attacks on the street. I'd just start wheezing and hyperventilating. My mother used to take me to school.

Everybody was riding the train to school and there I would be with my mother holding my hand, as if I were a toddler. When they saw that I was getting worse, not better, my parents put me in therapy.

"The therapists kept suggesting that they put me in a special school for troubled kids. I wasn't about to go to a school for kids with emotional problems so my parents arranged to get me a home tutor. I had to take all of these psychological evaluation tests. In order for the county to pay for the tutor, they had to figure out if I was really eligible. And—surprise, surprise—I was."

"So you stopped going to school?"

"Eventually. Then, on top of therapy, the home tutor, and my depression, I started dating this guy who was twenty-one years old. I was only fifteen. He and I went out for three years."

"Did your parents know?"

"Yeah, they found out. And they were pissed that I was dating someone that old. I guess I was pretty young. But even if he and I were the same age, my parents would have hated him all the same. He was from Argentina. He was a pathological liar, a drug dealer, I mean the whole nine, a total loser. All we ever did together was get high, have sex, and fight. But I was really into him. He was all that I really had. I couldn't deal with being at home and I couldn't deal with being outside of my home. I mean, if it weren't for that home tutor, I wouldn't have been able to graduate from high school."

"But Jade, you ended up getting it together. You went to college, didn't you?"

"For a hot minute. The first three years after I got out of

high school, I didn't do much of anything. It all depended on how depressed I was or wasn't. I went to different junior colleges; I went to therapy; I did the New York club scene, the downtown drug scene. I was all over the place. Around the same time that my folks moved down to D.C., I settled down and started going to school in Syracuse."

"The depression went away?"

"You could say that. My first year at school was amazing. I was heavily involved in political activism, always going to marches and rallies. I guess I was trying to funnel my rage into a productive activity."

"What were you so angry about?"

"Life, the world, God. I was just angry that my life turned out the way it did. Maybe the depression didn't really go away, not completely. But I met this guy, Gary, and for a while I was too busy being in love to be angry or sad. He and I went out for two years. He was a dream come true; we were a dream come true. I never thought anyone would love me, you know. But Gary did. He loved me a lot. I wish I could go back and stop my life right there, with Gary, in Syracuse. I was happy."

"What happened?"

"I got sick. He tried to cope. I got sicker. He tried harder. The sicker I got, the tighter I held on to him; he pulled away. And I came home where, chances are, I will live unhappily ever after unless . . ."

"Unless what?"

"Unless things change. What'd you call it the last time we were sitting here? 'The power of change.' Is that why you're moving back to L.A.? You need a change?"

"I'm suffocating here, Jade. It's a little too close to my past. Hey, why don't you come to L.A. with me? We could get a place together."

"Oh that'll be a real healthy living situation. Two depressed people staying up all night smoking cigarettes and talking about their glory days. We'd be like a ball and chain around each other's ankles. Anyway, moving doesn't help. Believe me, I've tried."

When the conversation died down, Jade insisted on going home. She said the night air and the drive would do her good. It was impossible for me to tell whether she was feeling any better. I was still concerned that she might try to commit suicide.

"Will you be alright?" I asked.

"I don't know, but I'll try to come by to see you again before you leave. Okay?"

"Yeah," I replied, feeling relieved. "That'd be great."

After she left, I had a fierce desire to write. I sat behind my computer and wrote the word *death* over and over, until it filled the monitor screen. Then I inserted *D.C.* randomly throughout the text. I pulled out the folder that contained my notes for *The Washington Post* article. I wrote a paragraph:

> There is history in this place. There are times when even the air weeps a eulogy for days past, things forgotten. Some days, I remember. . . . I have come in search of the new D.C., a city suspended somewhere between life and death.

Then I wrote a second paragraph, and a third. Before the sun came up, I had completed an entire essay.

Words had always been my source of freedom; they were my cure-all. But as I sat there writing, I began to wonder if words on a page would be enough to get me past my pain. Maybe Eugene was right; maybe I did need psychotherapy. I had always only thought of therapy in stark, clinical terms: an old bespectacled grey-haired white man with a couch in his office listening to the confessions of crazies. All of a sudden, this image didn't seem frightening, or threatening, anymore. What if, I asked myself, those "crazies" are no different than me? What if they are like me, ordinary people leading ordinary lives who woke up one day and discovered they couldn't get out of bed, no matter how much they wanted to or how hard they tried?

My past, my memories, my pain was more than I could bear. I needed someone to help me sort them all out. I had so many issues to deal with. More issues, as one of my friends says, than *People* magazine. And talking with my friends was out of the question. There were limits to what I was ready and/or willing to confide. I decided that when I got to L.A., I would give therapy a try. Why not? There was nothing to lose, everything to gain.

Possibilities

Through the many years and many relationships, my deepest spiritual yearning had been to reconnect with the source of my passion and, in so doing, finally to dispel my fear of being "crazy"—that is, passionate—in a world that treats passionate folks, especially women, as crazy. Only with strong spiritual confidence could I move through my fear of being crazy and learn simply to live.

—Carter Heyward

from *When Boundaries Betray Us*

THE WEEK AFTER Korama and I moved back to Los Angeles, my article ran in the Sunday edition of *The Washington Post*. Bryan, Jade, and Scott called to congratulate me. My father also called.

"I'm impressed," he said. "It was pretty good."

Had anyone else spoken those words, I would have been bubbling over with joy, but with my father, I found reason to be offended.

"What do you mean, you're impressed?" I asked, defensively. "You didn't think I could write?"

"Nana-Ama," he said stiffly, "I didn't say that. You and I both know that whenever you decide to do whatever it is you want to do with your life, you'll do it well."

Then he shut himself back up in his shell of silence, like a tortoise, protecting itself from further assault.

I waited for my mother to call, but as the day wore on, I grew tired of waiting, and decided to call her.

"Did you get the paper today?" I asked.

"Yes," she said.

"Did you read my article?"

"Yes," she said.

"So," I huffed impatiently, "did you like it?"

"It was really nice," she replied matter-of-factly. "You should mail a copy to Uncle Paul." I thought she was going to say something else about the article, something more heartening, more laudatory, but that was all. Dissatisfied, I fished for a more distinct compliment.

"My editor really liked the piece. He says I might be able to do another one pretty soon."

"That sounds great," she said. "Have you found a job yet?"

On Monday, when the out-of-town papers hit the L.A. newsstands, I picked up a copy of the *Post*. I thought that seeing my first major byline would make me feel some profound sense of achievement. It didn't. It merely added to my misery. What was it that I wanted to accomplish with my life?

I was working part-time as a personal assistant for a writer who also happened to be a friend. The job didn't pay a whole lot, but it was better than being unemployed. Korama was in preschool and Justin started picking her up for regular visits two evenings a week. Seeing him so frequently turned out to be a good thing. It was a constant reminder of how easily my life could spin out of control if I didn't keep my depression in check. Every moment I had was devoted to building a sturdy foundation.

By the end of March, I started to feel displaced; I wanted desperately to get my own place. I didn't bother to go apartment hunting because I knew it would be a wasted effort. My credit was bad and, even with the money I had saved from my job, I couldn't front a first, last, and security deposit. I called a former landlord who agreed to rent me a one-bedroom bungalow-style apartment on a deferred payment plan. He was the same landlord who came to my rescue after Justin threw me out. The apartment was teeny, less than seven hundred square feet, but it had a lot of character. There were six other bungalows in the complex, five of which were occupied by struggling artists.

Every day after work, I went by the apartment and walked through it, dreaming of all the wonderful things I would fill it with. The night before I was supposed to move in, I stopped by, as usual. The door was locked and my key, the same one I had used all those other nights, couldn't open it. Determined to get in, I kept trying the key, turning the knob, leaning my weight on the door, pushing, banging, until finally, three of the glass panes on the door shattered.

I walked across the small courtyard and knocked on a neighbor's door. A young, freckle-faced white man opened the door a crack and stuck his head out.

"Yes," he said, his reddish-blond hair falling into his eyes. I introduced myself and asked if I could use his phone to call the landlord. He looked at me suspiciously, said, "I guess," handed me a cordless phone and then shut the door in my face. Well, I thought as I dialed the landlord's number, he certainly won't be baking any pies to welcome me into the neighborhood. When I arrived the next morning with my belongings, the door had been repaired and my key was able to fit into the lock again.

After I was completely unpacked and feeling a bit settled, I began calling everyone I knew in town to let them know that I was back. My Rolodex, I soon discovered, was totally outdated. Most everyone I knew had moved or changed jobs. I called my friends on the East Coast to give them my new phone number and address. Jade was not home, but that was to be expected. I left a message on the machine and figured that she would get back to me when she was up to it. Everyone else I talked to was in the midst of some major life change: Bryan had joined the Peace Corps and was leaving for Budapest; Eugene was now living with his girlfriend; Scott was being evicted. And, on top of that, he had gotten into a fist fight, during which his nose was broken.

I had foolishly envisioned everyone going about the same routines, living the same lives they had been when I was there. It really threw me. Time was moving way too fast and though I was hell-bent on chasing it, I never could catch up. I always fell behind.

On April 5, 1993, a few days after we moved into our new apartment, Korama turned two. Her birthday amplified the sense of urgency I was feeling. When I looked at her, I didn't see a baby anymore. She was a little person who was maturing, growing bigger by the day. With the depression now gone, I was better able to meet her needs, which were also growing by the day.

However, money was tight. The rent and utilities got paid, and there was food in the house, but that was it. Korama had none of the luxuries other kids had. There were no fancy clothes, shiny toys, or exciting activities. These things may sound trivial, but when everybody in preschool except your child has seen the latest movie and owns the hot new toy, you can't help but to feel as if, on some level, you are failing her.

Finding a full-time job was harder than I imagined. I hadn't worked a regular full-time job since I was twenty years old. My hours of availability were limited because Korama had to be picked up from preschool by six every evening. I registered with temp agencies but ended up having to turn down all of the assignments that were offered to me. The public transit system in Los Angeles is, at its best, slow and unreliable. And the city is huge and sprawling. Without a car, it was impossible for me to get from a job to the preschool in time to pick Korama up.

I tried to reorient myself with the art world in hopes of finding a more flexible source of income. In late April, I created and mounted a theatrical piece. It was well-received but nothing concrete came out of it. I sent my resume and writing samples out to various magazines that I knew worked with freelancers. There were no immediate responses. You can only try so hard and do so much until, finally, you admit defeat.

My unhappiness underscored everything I did. On the days that I wasn't working my part-time job, I dropped Korama off at school, came home, and got back in bed. It was a relief to not have to move a muscle. I didn't leave the house unless it was absolutely necessary. I'd lie in bed and do nothing until even that felt like it was taking an excessive amount of effort. Then I would go outside and sit on my front stoop. That's how I came to befriend my neighbor, Harold Stanton, the one who had slammed his door in my face.

Harold usually came home on his lunch break and found me sitting there, staring off into space. Once, he invited me to join him for lunch and, after that, it became a regular event. He and I would sit in front of his television set with sandwiches in hand and watch *All My Children*. Sometimes after work, he would bang on my door and we would hop into his Miata and go grocery shopping together. To an extent, he and I assumed the same relationship that I'd had with both Scott and Bryan. He braced me with companionship. But unlike Scott and Bryan, Harold maintained very solid boundaries with me. He refused to be my rescuer. The deeper I fell into depression, the harder I tried to cling to him.

"Meri, you're really wearing me out," he once told me. "Why don't you get some help, go into therapy?"

Since arriving in Los Angeles, I hadn't given therapy a second thought. Having distanced myself—physically—from my past, therapy just wasn't a priority.

"I've considered it," I told Harold. "But I can't afford to right now."

"Seems to me," he said, "the way you're feeling, you can't afford not to."

In May, I borrowed some money from a friend and took a six-day trip to D.C. Bryan was leaving for Hungary in a few months and I wanted to spend some time with him. Mum was excited about seeing Korama and me. Every day before we left, she called to check, double-check, and triple-check our flight itinerary. On the day of our arrival, she left work early to prepare my favorite meal. I, too, was looking forward to seeing her. That's the way it usually worked with me, the farther away I was from my family the closer I felt to them.

Korama and I rode the subway from the airport to the station closest to The Ivy. Jade met us there and drove us the rest of the way. I hadn't even stepped over the threshold of the front door when my mother greeted me with a critical remark.

"Yuck," she said. "You're still wearing your hair like that?"

She was referring to my new crop of baby dreadlocks.

"You look like a pineapple from the neck up," she continued.

Paula was standing beside Mum. She cut her eyes at her and angrily rolled them skyward.

"Let it go," Jade whispered in my ear. "Take a deep breath and let it go."

"I think your hair looks dope, Nana-Ama," Paula said as she approached Korama and me. "It's growing so fast."

"Thanks Pooh," I said, entering the apartment. I gave Mum a small hug.

It never failed; the minute I walked into that house, I always went back to being sixteen and bitter.

While I was in town, my editor at *The Washington Post* took me to lunch. I used the opportunity to try to land another freelance assignment, but he hated all the ideas I pitched him. Mostly, we chatted about our personal lives. Several segues in the conversation landed us on the topic of phone sex. While trading stories about the weird jobs we had each had, I mentioned that I had once worked as a 976 operator. After hearing this, he wouldn't let the subject drop. He wanted me to tell all: how I had gotten involved in that industry, what kind of calls I had taken, how much I was paid, et cetera, et cetera.

"That's your article right there," he said, after I had filled him in on all the grisly details. I thought it was the funniest thing I had ever heard.

"My article? You mean like a day in the life of a 976 worker? You can't be serious."

"Why not?" he asked. "It would be a fascinating story."

Never in a million years would I disclose something so personal. I could see my mother's face already. She would flip if after all those years of teaching me to not put my business in the street, I got up and announced to the world that I had faked orgasms and simulated fellatio on the telephone for a living.

"I'm sure it would," I agreed. "But I'm not going to be the one to write it. My parents and friends live in D.C., They read the *Post*. I don't want anybody knowing I did that, least of all them."

"They'll get over it," he said. "The first shock is the hardest. Think about it, it'll be a great piece."

I agreed to think about it but, in my mind, I had pretty much decided that I wouldn't do it.

———

It was nice to spend time with all my friends. Everyone kept commenting about how much happier I looked and how L.A. must be treating me right.

"Oh, it is," I told them all. "I have never been happier in my life." Of course it was a lie, but the truth would have been a boring extension of the emotional hardships they had grown accustomed to hearing me talk about. It sickened me to hear myself complaining over and over again about the same problems. Problems that never went away; problems that apparently had no solutions. I sometimes wondered how many of them really listened anymore when I talked about my never-ending discontent.

Being with my friends so much left me little time to spend with Mum and Paula.

"This isn't the Holiday Inn," Mum complained. "It would be nice if you stayed in one night. Why can't your friends visit you here?"

She had a point. I took it for granted that I would see Mum and Paula because I was staying there. It wasn't intentional. If Mum hadn't brought it to my attention, I don't think I would have noticed. My family had become so peripheral to me that it seemed somewhat natural to pass by them without a second glance, as if they were permanent fixtures in a convenient corridor.

I ended up writing the article on my experience as a phone sex worker. It was the lead piece in the Sunday "Outlook" section of the paper. Both of my parents called and raved about it, curiously sidestepping any discussion of its content. How was it that the one thing I surely thought would bring them shame ended up legitimizing me as a writer in their eyes? No more questions about when I was going to get a job. No more lectures about how writing was a cute hobby but that I needed to have something to fall back on. I was now their daughter, the writer. Their sudden praise left me confused. Nevertheless, I seized their approval and wore it proudly.

In late June, I traveled to D.C. again. A friend had given me a frequent flyer award and I lied about Korama's age so that she could fly free as a lap child. It was a short trip; we arrived on Friday and left the following Monday. In that Sunday's "Outlook" section of the *Post*, there was an article about depression titled "In Black Despair." I almost didn't read it because when I saw the headline I assumed it was a personal essay by a white person and was immediately put off by the way *black* had been coupled with *despair*. I despise the way blackness, in the English language, symbolizes death and negativity. Because I believe that the absorption of these connotations contributes to self-hate, I avoid them at all cost.

However, when I noticed that the byline belonged to Mary Ann French, a black woman, I started reading the article. It was written on the heels of Washington, D.C., Council chairman John Wilson's suicide. French set out to examine the "plague of African American depression." Plague?!? And here I was thinking that Jade, Patricia Bledsoe, and I were anomalies. Never had I heard depression being referred to as an issue concerning African Americans, much less a plague. I was intrigued.

According to the article, John Wilson had hanged himself in his house. French quoted from one of Wilson's last speeches, which, ironically, was delivered at a meeting of the D.C. Mental Health Association. In that speech, he said, "Our kids are not crazy. They're not a generation of lost people. They're a generation of people that need mental health treatment to deal with depression because there's so much in this world that they can never have, and they know they will never have it, and it's putting them in a grand funk."

I thought back to what Paula had said about all the young kids that were dying; I wondered if mental illness factored in their deaths or the lifestyles that led them to early graves. I had recently read a lot of books about depression. All of the narratives contained elements that resembled my own experiences with the disorder. I often joked with Jade that sometimes when I looked at the author photos on the back of the books I half-expected to see her face or mine. But, of course, I knew that could never happen because all of the authors were white. Perhaps, unknowingly, what I was really trying to say was that I *wanted* to see her face or mine because depression was still viewed as a predominantly "white" illness.

The article affirmed the fact that there are indeed large numbers of black people suffering from depression. But why wouldn't there be? Depressive disorders do not discriminate along color lines, people do. People determine what is publicly acceptable and what is not, who may behave in what way at which time and under which circumstances;

and these social mores spill over into our private lives, into the images we create. White people take prescription drugs with gentle, melodic names; they go to therapy once or twice a week in nice, paneled offices. Black people take illicit drugs with names as harsh as the streets on which they are bought. We build churches and sing songs that tell us to "Go Tell It on the Mountain." Either that or we march. Left, right, left, from city to city, for justice and for peace. We are the walking wounded. And we suffer alone because we don't know that there are others like us.

Jade called to tell me about the article.

"Meri, there's a piece in the paper today. Did you—"

"Yeah," I interrupted. "I read it. What did you thin—"

"Good. Unbelievable," she said. "I've never . . ."

"Me neither," I whispered into her silence. "It was such a shock . . ."

"Unbelievable," Jade sighed. "I was so happy to see it."

"I know," I said, fighting back tears. "Me, too. I was happy, too."

My being in town at the same time that the article ran was simply too much of a coincidence to dismiss. I saw it as a sign to get my butt into therapy, to do whatever it took to get well. I clipped the article and folded it away into the side compartment of my purse. At the airport the next day, I pulled it out and re-read it as I awaited the final boarding call for our flight. Patricia Bledsoe came to mind. With all the political work she had done, she must have surely been acquainted with John Wilson. Perhaps they had even been friends. I wondered if either of them had known that the other was suffering from depression. Somehow, I doubted it. They probably ran into each other at different soirées and political functions, smiled hello or even chatted briefly, neither realizing that the other shared their private hell.

I walked to a pay phone and dialed Patricia Bledsoe's number. I hadn't seen or talked to her since Eugene's visit. For so long, he had been telling me to call her, talk to her. I didn't know what I was going to say, but I had an urge to reach out. Maybe I would talk to her about the article, ask her about John Wilson's death, anything. I just wanted to make a connection. After one ring, I lost my nerve. Before anyone could answer, I returned the phone to its hook and fetched my quarter from the coin return slot.

━━◆━━

WHILE EVERYONE IN L.A. basked in the summer sun, I became a hermit. My agoraphobia was worse than ever. I couldn't go out without getting anxious. But I wasn't despondent. I was, in fact, very productive. I got a few more freelance assignments. Harold let me use his computer while he was at work and before long, I completed the anthology and sent it off to my agent.

Paula came to spend her summer vacation with Korama and me. She and I were long overdue for some quality time. When she got there, I started to regret having invited her. My financial situation was still shaky and the apartment was much too small for three people. I was used to having the place all to myself when Korama was at preschool. I was moody and irritable. Paula walked on eggshells around me and did not speak unless it was in response to something I said. I nagged and fussed at her all day, every day, finding fault with everything she did. What especially irked me was that she woke up too late and stayed in bed too long.

Four long, miserable days into her vacation, we got into a huge blow-out. She had spent the afternoon in the bedroom watching soap opera after soap opera. I sat in the living room reading a book that I was supposed to review. The TV was too loud; I was having trouble concentrating on my work. Paula came out of the bedroom and went into the kitchen for a snack. She stood in front of the refrigerator and stared into it for a good long while before closing it and returning, empty-handed, to the bedroom. I could tell she was bored. I felt guilty about behaving so selfishly. The poor girl had come at my request. She had no friends in L.A., nowhere to go, nothing to do. It was cruel of me to let her sit around alone and lonely all day.

I went into the bedroom and watched the rest of the soap with her. When it was over, I turned off the television and asked her if she wanted to do something like take a walk down Melrose Avenue and windowshop.

"I don't feel like it," she said.

"Well, what do you feel like doing?" I asked.

"I'm cool doing what I was doing," she said, turning the television back on. My guilt turned to frustration. Her indifference frightened and infuriated me. She reminded me of myself when I was in the midst of a depressive episode.

"What the hell is wrong with you?" I asked. "You mope around here all day like a chained puppy that wants to be let out, then when I try to take you somewhere, you don't want to go."

Paula was astounded, but not intimidated. She kept direct eye contact as I ranted and raved about how I was doing my best and the least she could do was meet me half-way. When I was done, she said, in a spine-tingling voice, "You say you understand, but you don't. You are just like everyone else. I'm leaving."

"I am not like everyone else," I yelled, figuring that the everyone else she meant was our parents. "What's that sup-posed to mean, anyway?"

Paula didn't say another word. She went through the room, collecting her belongings and throwing them into her suitcase. I convinced her, with apologies and promises, to stay.

I had no idea that Paula also suffered from bouts of clin-ical depression. At the time, neither did she. What I did know was that as much as we cherished our relationship, it was hard for us to be together. My guess is that her sadness rubbed off on me, as I am sure mine did on her.

I went into therapy. It was the only sensible solution. The corner into which I had backed myself was getting too tight. I had been lying to my friends and family, telling them how incredibly happy and fulfilling my life in L.A. was. And they were all so proud of me. They thought I had finally found my way. I didn't want to break down and tell them the truth, that I was hurting, in a bad way. Even if I had wanted to, there was no one to talk to. All my friends were busy with their own lives and their own problems.

Now that Eugene was living with his girlfriend, he wasn't as accessible. Scott was in and out of court with his landlord every other week; and, as usual, Jade rarely returned my phone calls. David was not easy to reach. He was in Boston, working a grueling schedule as a broadcast news producer. Even if I was able to get a hold of him, I wouldn't know where to begin. He didn't know anything about my depressions. I had deliberately withheld that one tidbit of information from him. It just felt like too much to place on an already overloaded friendship. Besides, since seventh grade, he had done his fair share of listening to me.

I knew very little about psychotherapy, although I did hold the preconceived notion that it was an expensive indulgence. Hoping I could find something within my financial reach, I first tried the social services programs, many of which were geared toward low-income people, such as myself. All of the programs that I looked into had waiting lists of six months to two years and upwards. For someone suffering from depression, six months to two years might as well be a death sentence. I didn't want to wait.

Finding a private therapist in L.A. was a piece of cake. Next to plastic surgeons and personal trainers, they were the top miracle workers. It seemed as if everyone I met began at least one sentence in a conversation with, "My therapist says . . ." All I would have to do was wait for someone to make a remark about their therapist and then casually ask for a referral. I did and I struck oil on the first try. Someone referred me to a therapist whose fees were on a sliding scale.

I called the therapist, Sylvia Granderson. She informed me that the lowest rate she could offer was fifty dollars for a fifty-minute session. A dollar per minute! I was hoping her scale would slide a little further down than that. Fifty dollars was a small fortune for me, but I went ahead and made an appointment. My first visit with Sylvia was remarkable. She was a butch white lady in her early thirties. Her office, which was small and nondescript, was a stone's throw from my apartment. When I walked in the first thing I saw was a couch. It took every ounce of courage I had to not turn around and run. I nervously sat down and wrung my hands. Sylvia sat on the chair at her desk and swiveled it around so that she was facing me.

"Meri," she said in a tender, subdued voice, "do you want to tell me why you're here?"

I balled my hand into a fist, raised it up sideways to my mouth and coughed.

"I don't really know," I answered. "I might be a little depressed. I mean, I'm not feeling that great these days. What I'm trying to say is that I-I-I . . . I just need to talk to somebody."

"I'd like to help, if I can," she said with a smile. "What do you want to talk about?"

I felt idiotic sitting in front of a woman that I knew

nothing about, telling her that I wanted to talk. It was uncomfortable.

"I don't know. Nothing really."

"I want to hear about what you're going through and the reasons why you are here, but first I want to get some background so that I can have a clear picture of where you are in your life. Do you want to tell me about yourself?"

"Well," I hesitated. I didn't know what to tell her. It made me self-conscious to think that everything I said would be analyzed and scrutinized. I didn't want to say the wrong thing. I thought and thought about where to begin and then I saw the clock on her wall and remembered she was charging me by the minute. Ten had already flown by.

"Sure," I finally said. "I was born in Ghana. My whole family is from there. I came here when I was six. America that is, not L.A."

"Where did you grow up?"

It felt like I was on the witness stand being cross-examined. I was tense and on guard, but I slowly started opening up. I told Sylvia about most of my early childhood, especially about Auntie C. and Uncle Paul and how much I missed them. By the time she said our session was over, I was letting it all hang out. I was leaning back on her couch as if I were lounging in my living room. We scheduled another session for the next week. I wrote her a check and went home feeling happy and rejuvenated.

The next session was hard. Sylvia wanted me to talk more about my family. I started with Paula. I told Sylvia about how we had been able to turn around what had started out to be a horrible summer vacation. Besides Korama, I said, Paula was the most special person in my life.

"And your parents?" she asked.

"What about them?"

"What is your relationship like with them?" she asked.

"It's . . ." I couldn't think of an appropriate word. "It's there."

"There?" she asked. "You mentioned that they were divorced. Let's talk about them individually. What is your relationship like with your father?"

"We have an okay relationship," I said, and then quickly took it back. "That's not really true. We talk sometimes, but it's difficult. I've never forgiven him for leaving my mother, for leaving me."

"Have you told him how you feel?" she asked.

"Are you kidding?" I laughed. "I used to yell and cuss and scream at him so much when I was younger, it's a wonder he still talks to me." I leaned back and started untying my shoelaces. Suddenly I was feeling confined. "It was hard, you know, for my mother to raise two children by herself."

"It sounds like you're very protective of your mother," Sylvia said. "Tell me about her."

"She's . . . she's . . . ," My mind, my heart, everything shut down. I went blank.

"She was a good mother," I finally spit out. My throat was parched and my hands were trembling.

"Can I get some water?" I asked. Sylvia stepped out of the room and came back with a glass of water.

"Are you alright?" I nodded as I drank. "Do you harbor resentment and anger toward your mother as well?"

"No," I snapped. "Anger? Why would I be angry at her? She's all I've ever had." Then I started crying. I was sobbing so hard that my nose started running and a pain settled in my head, right between my eyes. "I don't feel like I really know her. She worked a lot. She had to. My father wasn't around and we needed the money. It was like after Daddy left, we weren't a family anymore. We were just there. How could I be angry at her for that? It wasn't her fault."

I couldn't stop crying. My head felt like a huge water bubble that was about to explode. I had gone from feeling nothing at all, to being overloaded with emotions I didn't understand. Sylvia handed me a tissue and gave me a moment to regain my composure. My full-lunged gasps were soon replaced by slower, calmer breaths. I was so embarrassed about breaking down like that, I couldn't even look at Sylvia. I stared at the pink triangle charm hanging on her necklace.

"I'm sorry," I said. "I don't know what came over me. I seem to be crying over the dumbest things lately."

"You don't have to apologize," she said. "It's quite alright. We can continue this discussion next week. Before we end this session, I want you to tell me how you've been feeling. Last week you said that you thought you might be depressed. Tell me about how you generally feel from day to day."

I started crying again.

"I'm tired," I told her through the tears. "I'm so tired of

everything. I feel like I just want the world to stop spinning for a while so I can take a break."

She turned to her desk and wrote down something on a sheet of paper.

"I don't know how much you know about depression," she said, handing me the paper. "but it is a medical condition, a disease. However, depression is treatable. Psychiatrists are medical doctors who specialize in the field of mental health; they can prescribe medication. I'm a psychologist. These are a few of the doctors that I sometimes work with. I want you to go and get an examination from one of them before our next session. They'll talk to you and decide which antidepressant will be best for you."

"Antidepressant?" I asked. All I wanted to do was get therapy, talk through my problems. I felt like I had failed some sort of test. Maybe I shouldn't have brought up the word depression. "You want me to take Prozac?"

"Prozac is not the only antidepressant," she explained. "There are many, many others. I am sure the psychiatrist will go over all your options with you."

"Okay," I said, glancing at the names she had written down. It was pointless to ask her anymore questions. There were few things I despised more than going to the doctor, and taking medicine was one of them. Asking someone who doesn't even take aspirin to take medication that will alter her brain chemistry is like asking an atheist to go on a pilgrimage to Mecca. I stuffed the sheet of paper in my purse and put my shoes back on. I was dizzy with regret. What had I done? It had all been a big mistake; going there, telling her all my business, bawling like that. This woman probably thought I was a complete basket-case. I was seized with feelings of shame. I paid my money and left. That was the last session I had with Sylvia.

In late August, I found a job. It was as the Membership/Program Coordinator for PEN Center USA West, the writers' organization. Based on the job description, I thought it was going to be a high-level position but it turned out to be nothing more than a secretarial job with a big title. To top it off, the work atmosphere was stifling. I hated being there, but I desperately needed the money.

Because cars are such a necessity in Los Angeles, I used the first few paychecks I got to buy one, a red 1983 Mazda 626. It ended up being my home away from home. At 7:30 I would wake up and from that moment on, I was on the go. Korama had to be dropped off at preschool by 8:30 so that I could get to work by 9:00. When my workday was over at 5:30, I would drive crosstown, pick Korama up at 6:00 and head home to fix dinner and finish up whatever freelance article I was writing. The routine was exhausting. I felt like a hamster on a treadmill. A few weeks of doing this set me back into a struggle against fatigue. The depression returned. With it came the insomnia, the disorientation, and the self-criticism.

When push came to shove, I beat up on myself for not being able to get with the program. After all, I'd tell myself, I was not the first woman to work and raise a child simultaneously. Black women have been doing that for ages, with and without partners. Some even held down two jobs while raising three and four children. No one ever made mention of these women griping about depression. It was a luxury that they couldn't afford. What made me think I was so special?

In the evenings while I was lying in bed, trying to invent ways to make myself fall asleep, I thought about going back to therapy. But not with Sylvia. If I could find another reasonably priced therapist who wouldn't attempt to push shrinks and pills on me, I might just give it a second try. For several days I tossed the idea around in my head. The final decision was no, I would not see another therapist. There wasn't an hour to spare in my schedule and fifty bucks was too much money to spend to hear myself talk about myself. Besides, my friends were still there. True, they weren't impartial or licensed, but they listened and they cared. Especially Jade. She did more than console or empathize, she knew. She knew firsthand.

When I called Jade, her sister, Monica, answered. Jade wasn't home so Monica took a message and said she would pass it on to Jade.

"It might be a while before she gets back to you," she said.

"Is she out of town?" I asked. I told Monica to let Jade know that it was urgent.

"Oh," she sighed. There was a pause on the other end of the phone.

"Monica?" I asked. "Are you still there?"

"Yeah. I was thinking that . . . I guess I can tell you. Jade is, uhm, she's . . ."

Jade was in a mental hospital. She had voluntarily checked herself in and was going to be there indefinitely.

"I'll give you the number there," Monica said. "I'm sure she'd love to hear from you."

Her words slowed and slurred in my ears, like a tape on the wrong speed. Jade? In a mental hospital?

"Is she okay?" I asked.

"Yeah, she's doing fine."

It was a stupid answer to a stupid question. Fine? How could she be doing fine if she was in a mental hospital? I was bending over backward trying to figure out why Jade would check herself into the loony bin. It was too difficult for me to believe that she was that far gone. Not that I had ever taken Jade's depression lightly. One of the things that I admired—and envied—most about her was that she was honest and up-front about it. Whenever she told me she was "going through it," I cleared the way and gave her space. Jade had an immense expanse of sadness. I understood that. I even partially understood her impulse for suicide. But hospitalization?

"She's doing *fine*?" I asked skeptically.

"As fine as she can be doing under the circumstances," Monica said. "Call her."

Monica gave me the number to the hospital and told me the best times to call. The thought of calling a mental hospital made me uncomfortable. I pinned the number up on my corkboard, knowing that sooner or later I would have to make the call. Had Jade been in the hospital for any other reason, I would have dialed that number without a second's hesitation, but since the cause for her admission was depression, it scared me. After months of pointing out the concentricity of our lives, I felt quite justified in my fear. Less than a year before, Jade had sat in my living room and said, "I'm not crazy. Well, no more than you." And I had believed her, because when I looked at her, it was so easy to see myself. God, if she was sick enough to be hospitalized, what did that say about me?

The next day I forced myself to make the call. My fear was secondary to my love. If I was ever in a similar situation, I would hope that my friends would be there for me. I expected a nurse to answer the phone, but the voice on the other end was Jade's. She didn't sound any different from her usual self.

"Jade?" I asked.

She recognized my voice right away.

"Meri," she crooned excitedly.

I pictured her lying on a twin-sized bed with starched white sheets in a room with white rubber walls and a white plastic coated telephone with a short, tangled cord glued to a white plastic nightstand. All that whiteness was blinding.

"They give you guys your own phone lines?"

No hello, how are you doing, just a straight nose dive into the Bedlam and Thorazine questions.

"No," she laughed. "I'm in the phone room, which is actually a hallway. This isn't Club Med, you know. It's good to hear your voice. How are you?"

"I'm doing fine. How are you?"

"Fine."

Talk about social axioms. Neither of us was fine. I had

prepared myself for Jade to be reticent, catatonic, or maybe even heavily sedated. She did sound subdued, but not alarmingly so.

"How're those palm trees?"

"Beautiful as ever," I said, staring at the one outside my window.

"I heard you've been calling. I'm sorry I haven't called you back. I've been—"

"Going crazy?" I asked. It was probably an inappropriate thing to say, but if Jade had been able to joke that night when she was planning to commit suicide, I couldn't imagine her not being able to now.

"This from the mouth of Miss Contrary herself," Jade laughed.

"Hey, which one of us is wearing the straitjacket, huh?" We jumped into our regular comical groove, as if all was well, as if we were sitting on the floor in my Mt. Pleasant living room drinking Heinekens, breathing in the smoke from our cigarettes, and letting the memories of our pasts swirl around us.

Before we got off the phone, Jade made me promise that I would get back into therapy. I gave her my word and, despite my reservations, I kept it. Seeing a therapist paled in comparison to being in a psych ward. I called Cedars-Sinai, the hospital where Korama was born, to see what type of mental health programs they offered. Cedars was known for its substance abuse programs. I figured that any place that dealt with addiction had to also offer therapy. I registered at Thalians, Cedars' mental health clinic, which, thankfully, offered a sliding payment scale. I paid twenty-two dollars and fifty cents for each visit.

Apparently, a good number of the therapists at Thalians were in training, and their session hours went toward their certification process. Incoming patients were assessed in a preliminary session and then routed off, based on their condition or problem, to a therapist who specialized in that particular field. Getting to therapy was tricky for me. Timing was an unconquerable obstacle. My regular child-care was during standard business hours. Evening sessions meant finding after-hours child-care. Daytime sessions meant taking a two-hour lunch. Either way, being in therapy was going to cost me a lot of money, above and beyond the session fee.

Shelly, the first therapist I saw, was a young, white, Australian woman. Her accent endeared her to me. It reminded me of Uncle Paul and Uncle Peter. As loving as that association was, it held me back from being totally open. I was too ashamed of my weakness, my morose feelings. Uncle Paul had expected nothing but the best for and from his "dah-ling Mildred." If Shelly was remotely like him, then she too would be confounded by the image of me as a dispirited woman.

My visits with Shelly were more like an afternoon tea with a friend, except, of course, I was paying to be there. She and I discussed my writing, my family, my romances, and the weather. I kept silent about the tedious turmoil that was knotting up my insides. One afternoon I arrived at Shelly's office looking as horrible as I felt. I had called in sick to work. My eyes were red from crying and lack of sleep; my head hurt so bad it felt like someone was drilling a hole in it.

"I can't do this anymore," I cried. "I need help."

"What's going on? Talk to me about it," she said, her intonations curling upwards with surprise.

"I'm talked out, lady. I haven't had a good night's sleep in weeks; I can't eat; I can't concentrate. What can you possibly say in the next forty-five minutes that will change that? I don't even know why I bothered to come today."

I picked up my things to leave.

"Where are you going?" she asked.

"I'd say hell, but I'm already there. You'll excuse me if I'm not up to chatting today."

"Wait," she said, picking up the telephone. "Don't leave. Let me page the psychiatrist on duty. He might be able to help you."

I stayed. Not because I wanted to, but because I couldn't leave. I couldn't make myself get up. I couldn't find one good reason. If I did leave, where would I go? What would I do? Everywhere I had been, everything I had tried up to that point had landed me back in the same place, confronting the same depression. I was fed up with the whole pattern. Prior to that day, I was adamant about not taking medicine. It was a remedy that, to me, was worse than the ailment. I don't know what changed my mind. People find faith in the most peculiar ways. It might have had something to do with Jade being in the hospital. Or it might have been that I was determined to do whatever it took to end my pain, be it drugs or be it death. Whatever it was, it took hold of me. I stayed and waited for that psychiatrist to come.

Dr. Fitzgerald, the psychiatrist, did not physically examine me. Not that day, or any other day. Based only on my description of the symptoms I was experiencing, he told me that I should be taking an antidepressant. Dr. Fitzgerald explained that once I started taking the pills, it could take anywhere from two to six weeks for them to take effect, but when they did, the physical symptoms of depression would be alleviated. He warned me of the potential side effects—dry mouth, excessive yawning, possible weight gain, and a multitude of other things that seemed, at the time, a small sacrifice for the freedom I would have from depression.

After I signed a consent form, Dr. Fitzgerald wrote out a prescription for Zoloft, an antidepressant drug in the same family as Prozac. When I told him I couldn't afford to have the prescription filled right away, he gave me ten sample packages. I took the small boxes of medicine and walked out of the clinic believing that soon, all my troubles would be behind me.

FOR THE FIRST WEEK, I took one 50-milligram pill of Zoloft each morning. In the second week, I followed Dr. Fitzgerald's instructions and doubled the dosage to 100 milligrams. As forewarned, I suffered from dry mouth and yawning. The medicine also made me feel woozy and lightheaded. I had this sensation of experiencing the world through a dream-like haze, like I had stepped into a painting. These side effects only lasted a couple of weeks and then they disappeared, taking with them my ability to experience any emotions in extremity. Except anxiety. I stayed uncontrollably nervous and edgy.

I had always thought that the opposite of depression was happiness, that once you stopped feeling bad, you automatically started feeling good. That's not what happened to me. Once I started taking Zoloft, there was no good or bad, I just stopped feeling. It was like being glued on top of the fence that separated pain from pleasure; nothing could transport me to the other side, either side. My mind could no longer access my heart, even in circumstances that would have ordinarily moved me to tears or laughter.

When I met with Dr. Fitzgerald again, I told him all about it. In addition to my weekly therapy sessions with Shelly, I had one session with Dr. Fitzgerald every two weeks so that he could monitor my response to the medication. He offered an explanation for my dulled emotions.

"Some patients," he said, "react to Zoloft that way. The medication prevents them from reaching extreme lows, but it also prevents them from reaching extreme highs. I wouldn't worry too much if I were you. It's perfectly normal. It may pass. Let's give it some time."

"Alright," I said, "but there's another problem. The Zoloft's making me really jumpy. I feel like I just drank two pots of super strong coffee."

For my uncontrollable nervousness, Dr. Fitzgerald offered more medication. He gave me a prescription for

BuSpar, an anxiety controllant. Because I couldn't afford to fill that prescription either, he gave me sample packages. Damn, I thought, more pills. How many damn pills would I have to swallow before I felt like a regular person again?

The financial strain that treating the depression put me under was enough to push me into a whole new depression. Seeing Shelly cost $22.50 a week; Dr. Fitzgerald's visits cost $13.00 each. When I ran out of the sample packages of Zoloft, I filled the prescription, which was for thirty-days' worth of pills. It cost me a little under $75. Had I filled the prescription for BuSpar, that would have cost me $130, but I didn't. When the BuSpar samples ran out I found another way to treat the anxiety—alcohol. It got the job done and it wasn't as hard on the pocket.

While I was taking Zoloft, I wasn't able to write a word, much less a poem or essay, unless I was drinking. It's difficult to be passionate or polemic when you're desensitized. Whereas before I had been drinking to shield myself from the pain, now I was drinking to access the pain. I did tell Dr. Fitzgerald about my drinking, and he, predictably, told me to stop, explaining that alcohol was a depressant, that it would only reverse the effects of the antidepressant. But how could I stop? Two decades of my life had been spent addicted to one stage or another of depression. I paid Dr. Fitzgerald no mind. I needed my pain; I needed my depression to create, to live. So I drank. Never in my life had I drunk so much. It went from a modest desire into a craving, and progressed until it was a flesh and blood jones. Without the alcohol, my hands trembled and my feelings flatlined.

In her essay "Moving Targets: Alcohol, Crack and Black Women,"* Sheila Battle, MSW, claims that "studies show a higher prevalence of 'escape alcoholism' among black women. In other words, drinking that numbs them from the many griefs, sorrows and disappointments that color black female lives. . . . [B]ecause they often have full responsibility for their families and feel they must carry on no matter what, black women are even more likely to minimize the negative impact of alcohol in their lives." In my mind, drinking was helping, not hurting, me. Soon enough though, it tore my world to shreds.

I resigned from my job at PEN. I made the mistake of being honest with my boss and telling her that I was being treated for clinical depression. The woman never looked at me the same way again. It was a crash course on stigmatization. All of a sudden, my performance came under fire. I was not, she informed me, handling the stress and pressure of the position well. But that was not the only reason working there became unbearable. I was tired of being treated like a low-level clerk. Although my title was Membership/Program Coordinator, my supervisor demanded that I not fraternize with the members, some of whom were friends as well as colleagues. At events that we sponsored, rather than greet and assist the members as specified in my job description, I was made to lay out silverware and serve cold drinks.

*The Black Women's Health Book, edited by Evelyn C. White. Seattle, WA: Seal Press, 1994, p. 252.

It was demeaning and demoralizing. The Zoloft may have wiped out my rage, but it was helping restore my self-esteem.

My former job as a creative writing instructor became available. Rebecca Freemont, the writer who took over when I moved back to D.C., was relocating to New York. I reapplied for the position. It was just part-time teaching, but it was better than nothing. Two nights a week, I left Korama with a babysitter and drove to Manhattan Beach, California, to teach. Rebecca also let me lease her house, a two-bedroom with a white picket fence and a small backyard. It was an opportunity I couldn't pass up. The money I would be receiving for teaching my workshops was a hundred dollars shy of the monthly rent. I wasn't sure how I was going to make up the difference, or pay for my other bills, but, in prime Meri fashion, I took the leap and waited to see whether I would fall or fly.

On Halloween of 1993, Harold and I packed up my apartment and drove the boxes across town to yet another new residence. While putting away the bags of perishables that Harold had brought in his carload, I found an unopened bottle of vodka in the freezer. I didn't drink hard liquor so I handed it to Harold.

"No thanks," he said, returning it to me. "I'm not a big vodka drinker. I don't really need to have that lying around my house."

"Just take it," I demanded, shoving the bottle back into Harold's hands. "At least you drink it sometimes. I don't drink it at all. It burns going down. Might as well be sterno."

Harold opened the freezer and put the bottle back in.

"I'll grab it before I leave."

Of course he left without the vodka, and it stayed in the freezer, untouched, for many months.

To compensate for the isolation of living so far from my friends, every month I threw a party at my new house. When one party was over and done with, I spent the next three weeks preparing for the next one. It kept me occupied and out of trouble. It was also a way to make sure that my name was still floating through the artists' circle. So much of the networking and contact-making that artists do takes place at social events. Because I was at home with a child, there was no way I could attend the readings, premieres, and other functions to which I was invited. When Korama was an infant, I brought her along to these events, but as she grew older and refused to sit still, it became more and more of a hassle to negotiate the logistics of taking her. Hosting parties was an effort to stay connected. It also, I might add, made for pleasurable drinking.

At the end of the year, Shelly finished her training. When I began therapy no one at the clinic cared enough to fill me in on the fact that I would lose the one person with whom I felt comfortable enough to confide. Being that a good number of people in therapy are tackling issues of abandonment, one would imagine that a clinic's administrators would advise prospective patients that their therapist could pick up at any minute and leave. I went to a session with Shelly and found out that it would be our last. She had taken a position with a therapy center in Santa Monica. Shelly told me that because of the nature of the therapist/patient relationship, she was able to offer me the option of continuing treatment with her at her new place of employment. It all sounded well and good until she told me that her new fee at her new place of employment would be a staggering $150 an hour.

"If you decide to continue here," she said, "you'll be reassigned to a new therapist. I don't know who it'll be, but all the residents here are caring and competent."

Caring and competent? What were we talking about here, plumbers? She was acting like she could be replaced with anybody who was qualified to do the job. I wanted to slap her. I wanted to take back every confession, every intimate moment I had ever shared with her. While I understand the intellectual premise behind teaching hospitals where trainees can receive "hands-on" experience with patients, I fail to understand how an institution can thrust one therapist after another onto its clients and not expect them to be negatively affected. In the three months that I had been seeing Shelly, we had settled into a safe, trusting relationship. She knew so much about me. Had I not been so neutralized by the medication, I would have surely wept.

"I don't want to start all over again with someone else," I told her. "I don't care how caring or competent they are. They don't know me."

"Your next therapist will have background notes," she assured me. "It'll probably take just two or three sessions for them to get up to speed."

Notes? My life was being reduced to notes? I had never even seen Shelly taking notes during our sessions. In my mind, I could picture my prospective therapist eating corn chips at her desk while flipping through a folder full of hastily collected afterthoughts about me. Assuming that my new therapist was a woman. It could very well be a man. That got me thinking: Would my new therapist be black or white? Foreign or American-born? A parent or childless? These were important questions about even more important details. Shelly had no answers.

"I don't know," she said. "But if, for some reason, you don't like him or her, you can request to be reassigned."

"Reassigned?" I shouted. "What if I don't like the next person? Do I ask to be reassigned again? I could spend the next year trying out new therapists. And let me guess, I'm supposed to pay for it all, too. That's really fucked up, you know."

"Meri," Shelly pleaded, "please don't let this stop you from moving ahead with your therapy. You've been making great progress."

"No," I sighed. "*We*'ve been making great progress. No matter what kind of professional lingo you try to veil this with, it basically boils down to the fact that you're walking out on me. You're leaving, just like everyone else in my life has."

Shelly knew as well as I did that I would not return the next week to meet the new therapist. That seemed to trouble her more than it did me. I could see it in her eyes; I could hear it in her voice. All the training in the world could not have prepared her for this moment, for all the moments when she realized that despite her expert detachment, she had grown to care about her clients; she was just as attached to us as we were to her. It was obvious that saying goodbye was hard for her, too.

Shelly's departure left me feeling wounded and betrayed. How exactly does one mourn the loss of one's therapist? It's not like losing a friend or a lover. There is nothing to validate the emptiness that you feel inside; no poems, no songs on the radio, no made-for-TV specials. When you think about it, there is nothing really to affirm the depth of the relationship you once had or, that it was even a relationship at all. Relationships are based upon some sort of reciprocity. Generally, therapy is treated as a paid association, an agreement, not an authentic human relationship. So what if your therapist gets ill, takes a new position elsewhere, or drops dead? Big deal. Take your Kleenex, your checkbook, your dysfunctions, and go find another therapist. That was the message everyone seemed to be sending me.

My case was reassigned to a new therapist, but I didn't show up for my appointment. I did, however, continue taking the Zoloft and seeing Dr. Fitzgerald. I also continued to drink. The only time that I felt like myself, the self with which I was familiar, was when I was under the influence of alcohol. I became a pro at self-medicating. I found that if I measured the amount of alcohol I took in, I could manipulate my body to the point where I was fully functional, but not fully depressed.

All urban black neighborhoods are polluted with cheap liquor stores. The one in which I lived was no exception.

There were three within a four-block radius. They became my main haunts. Everyday, I went and bought a six-pack of beer. When I couldn't afford the brand-name beers, I experimented with cheap, drink-alone-sized bottles of wine, which smelled like nail polish remover and made me sick. Since I no longer worked a nine-to-five, my schedule was free and clear during the days. In the mornings after I dropped Korama off at preschool, I usually returned home and had a drink or two or six. That was the only way I could bring myself to sit down and write. One day after I had returned from dropping Korama, Paula called—collect. I had emptied the contents of my purse on the floor and was sitting there counting the change to see if I could swing a six-pack.

"This is not a good time," I told Paula. "I'm in the middle of something important."

"I'm sorry," she said. "I really need to talk to you."

"What's wrong, Pooh? Why aren't you in school?"

I was jittery. My throat was parched and itchy. All I wanted was to feel an ice cold liquid sliding into it. I picked up two quarters from the pile of coins and placed them one on top of the other, then I started picking out the nickels.

"I am at school," she answered. "It's lunchtime."

"How's school?" I asked, feigning interest.

"It's okay. The reason I called is that I wanted to ask you a question. I started going to therapy, you know, 'cause I've been feeling so bad . . ."

She paused for a response. I remained inattentive.

"Uh-huh," I mumbled. I placed the twelve nickels that I found in a stack next to the quarters and started looking for dimes.

"Anyway," Paula continued, "my therapist wants to put me on this medicine. She says that she can't do it unless she has legal consent from an adult. Mommy and Daddy don't know about it yet. I was wondering what you thought. Have you ever heard of . . . wait a second . . . let me get this piece of paper."

"Uh-huh," I repeated. There were only five dimes. That, in combination with the single dollar bill I had in my hip pocket, would barely buy me a pack of cigarettes. "Here it is," Paula said. "It's called Zoloft."

Hearing that word brought me to attention. I dropped the pennies that were in my hand and sat up straight.

"Did you say Zoloft?" I asked. "What about Zoloft? I'm lost. Can you start from the beginning again?"

Realizing that I hadn't been listening, she let out a sigh and begrudgingly repeated her story.

Inspired by a lengthy and crippling period of depression, Paula, who was seventeen at the time, had taken the initiative to find a therapist. She ended up going to a low-cost health facility. The therapist who met with her was so impressed by her courage and conviction that she reduced the clinic's fee to one dollar per visit so that Paula would be able to afford sessions. After several visits, the therapist diagnosed her as being clinically depressed and recommended that she take antidepressants.

There is no way to describe how I felt when I heard Paula talk to me about her own battle with depression. I was sad; I was furious; I was concerned; I was frightened.

Two people—two sisters—in the same family were being debilitated by the exact same disease. What did that mean? Was it bad genes or bad luck? Or a bad combination of both? It didn't matter. There was little solace in realizing that the illness might be genetic. A profound sadness moved through me. Even those pills that I dutifully swallowed every morning were not a strong enough barricade against the agony.

If there was ever a time when Paula needed my honesty, it was then. I told her that I, too, had received the same diagnosis and was taking Zoloft. She was as stunned by my confession as I had been by hers. I hadn't told anyone in our family about my illness. Like the sexual abuse, it remained my secret. My conversation with Paula was cut short because the lunch bell rang summoning her to return to class.

When she got home from school, she called me back, and we spoke at length.

"Does Mum know?" I asked her.

"Not yet," she said.

"Are you going to tell her?" I wanted to know.

"I have to. That's the only way I can get this prescription filled. Are you going to tell her about you?"

"I don't think so," I said. "At least, not for a while."

Through the static of the ten years and three thousand miles that stood between us, we discussed symptoms, psychiatrists, side effects, and suicide attempts.

As we shared our feelings, Paula and I bonded in much the same way that Jade and I had bonded during our first conversation about depression. There is a comfort that comes from talking to someone who is or has "been there." It provides you with a lens through which you can examine your own inner struggle. The illness so quickly clouds one's memories and perceptions that it's easy to lose track of the details of your suffering, the incidents that triggered an episode, which symptom came first, how long the episodes were, what past pleasures had been relinquished.

I never thought that one day my sister and I would be adding clinical depression to the list of things we had in common. Never could I have imagined that I would hear my sister say, "Me, too," in response to my explanations of the feelings I'd felt, the dismal places they had taken me. I would have given all the money I had, all those pennies, nickels, dimes, and quarters spread out before me, to make it not so.

Whatever heroic desires I might have had to rescue my sister from the rising tides of her sadness were thoroughly dwarfed by the magnitude of my own self-pity. At that point, I was very dedicated to the outdated theory of endogenous and exogenous depression, as if nature were not heavily influenced by nurture and vice versa. Anyhow, Paula's depression stood as proof positive for me that my own depression was most likely biochemical. That conclusion did me in. It confirmed my greatest fears; I was, as they say, "one sandwich short of a picnic." The horror of that thought sent me spiraling back into my pre-Zoloft existence.

Several dreary days went by before I went in for my regular appointment with Dr. Fitzgerald. When I mentioned to him that the medication wasn't working anymore, he increased the dosage I was taking from 100 milligrams to 150. I also told him about my conversation with Paula.

"That was a pretty traumatic discovery, wouldn't you say? I'm sure it touches on a lot of sensitive issues. You should discuss it with your therapist."

"My what?" I asked, kicking the heel of my right shoe against the couch. It was against the clinic's policy to dispense meds to clients who were not actively involved in psychotherapy. I had never bothered to reschedule a session with my new therapist.

"You seem a little anxious," Dr. Fitzgerald observed. "Are you taking the BuSpar?"

"Yes," I lied, planting my feet firmly on the carpet. I was embarrassed to admit that I couldn't afford to have the prescription filled.

"Have you stopped drinking?"

I nodded and smiled, thinking that I could use a drink right about then to calm my jitters. Our meeting took all of twenty minutes, after which time Dr. Fitzgerald handed me a new prescription for Zoloft and walked me to the door.

I was supposed to meet Eugene after my session with Dr. Fitzgerald. He had given a lecture in San Diego and decided to make a pit stop in L.A. on his way back to Minnesota. When he was setting up his itinerary, we made plans to spend one of the three days he was going to be in town together. That seemed like an eternity ago. Now that the time had arrived, I didn't much feel like being in anyone's company, but I had to go. A last-minute cancellation would only rouse suspicion, especially with Eugene.

After I left the clinic I drove to the liquor store and bought a small bottle of vodka, like the kind they sell on airplanes. I then went to a drive-through McDonald's, ordered a large cup of juice, tossed half of it out onto the grass, and poured in the vodka. By the time I arrived at the hotel where Eugene was staying, I was lit. I could see him through the plate glass window, pacing the lobby floor. As I walked through the front door, Eugene approached me with open arms.

"Hey," I said, kissing him on the cheek.

He backed away from me and grimaced.

"What's wrong?" I asked.

"Nothing," he said, giving me a hug. "Nothing at all. What time is it?"

"Ten-thirty. I know, I know, I'm late. What else is new?" I held up my keys and jingled them in the air. "Ready?"

Like most people who have had one too many, I wasn't aware of my own level of intoxication. I was certainly much too tipsy to be behind the wheel of a car. Eugene grabbed my arm.

"We don't have to leave so soon. We can go up to my room and catch up."

"I don't want to hang out in a hotel room. I thought you were treating me to breakfast."

"It's too late for breakfast. Let's wait until noon and have lunch."

With the utmost precision, Eugene coaxed me into spending the next two hours with him at the hotel, which was as basic and no-frills as a Motel 6.

"Do they have room service here?" I asked when we got up to his room. "I want to order a drink."

"Nope, but even if they did, it's a little early to drink," he said. "Some people are finishing their first cup of coffee."

"I guess you're right," I agreed.

He got up and poured me a cup of water from a pitcher that was on top of the dresser. We sat down on his bed and talked about everything under the sun except drinking and depression. It was one of those ask-me-no-questions-I'll-tell-you-no-lies scenarios. Finally at twelve-thirty, I jumped up and grabbed my purse.

"I'm starving, Eugene. Let's go eat."

He tried to keep stalling, but I insisted. When we got to the car, I unlocked the passenger door for him. He held on to the handle and exhaled.

"Maybe we could go somewhere around here. Aren't there restaurants in walking distance?"

I drove to a cafe on Melrose Avenue because it was close to Korama's preschool. I was fiending for a drink. When the waiter came to our table, I ordered a beer with my meal. Eugene frowned but said nothing. I got up and went to the bathroom. When I returned our lunch had been served. I was so hungry that I didn't notice until we were about to pay the check that the waiter never brought my beer. Eugene and I wasted away the rest of the afternoon strolling through the shops along the avenue.

Korama, Eugene, and I went back to the house. Korama watched a movie in her room. Eugene sat close beside me like a parent sits beside a feverish infant, looking on tenderly, with hope and disquiet reservation. Spending time with a depressed person is enervating. It is as dangerous as standing at the slippery edge of a precipice. When Eugene looked at me, I wondered whether what he saw brought back memories of his childhood and his mother's illness during that time.

"How's your mom?" I asked.

"It's winter," was all he said. And, indeed, that was all he had to say. We sat in an awkward silence for some time. I wondered why, after all he had been through with his mother, Eugene welcomed another depressive into his life. Wasn't he afraid of the consequences? How did he escape the contagious effects of mental illness?

"I guess I'm just lucky," he said, brushing off my questions with a slow wave of his hand and a fast change of the subject.

After dinner, I gave Korama her bath and put her to bed. I expected to come back to the living room and find Eugene waiting for me, armed with the questions and remarks he had been saving all day. Excluding the subject of his mother—which was raised by me—he hadn't said word one to me about therapy, medication, or anything else concerning mental health. That wasn't his style. But when I went into the room, he was curled up on my couch, deep into sleep. I woke him up and asked if he wanted me to call him a cab; he said that he was fine where he was. I covered him with a blanket, relieved that I had been spared the task of recounting my recent calamities.

I climbed into bed and stared at the ceiling for hours. I doubt that there is anything more annoying than wanting to fall asleep and not being able to. I got up and tip-toed into the kitchen to fix myself a drink with my ever-faithful bottle of vodka. A wave of panic came over me when I remembered that Korama had finished off the orange juice with dinner. I searched the refrigerator like a thief, hoping to find a suitable replacement, but came up with only milk and water. I rummaged through the cupboards and found something that looked like it might work—canned peaches. I opened the can and, using my fingers, pulled each peach slice out and tossed it into the sink. The syrup in the tin was thick. I didn't bother transferring it into a cup. I poured water and vodka into the syrup, stirred and drank straight from the tin.

I moved through the dark kitchen as quietly as a mouse so as not to wake Eugene. I wouldn't have known what to say if he had found me there in my pajamas, clutching a can filled with vodka, water, and peach syrup. This is truly pitiful, I thought; you are an alcoholic.

"So I am," I whispered into the darkness. The gravity of the admission hit me after it slipped out of my mouth. If I was an alcoholic, that meant I would have to join A.A. and give up alcohol forever. Forever! No more beers in the middle of a sweltering July. No more mimosas at Sunday brunch. No more red wine with pasta. Damn, how had it come to this? No, I thought, I'm not an alcoholic. Here I was, someone who didn't like hard liquor, pressing my lips into the jagged blades of a hard metal rim for a taste of booze. If that wasn't alcoholism, then what was?

I polished off the last of the vodka, but still didn't fall asleep. If I learned anything that night it was that insomnia is far worse to contend with when you're drunk. At about half-past six, I heard Eugene walking around the house. It was music to my ears. I threw off the covers and ran into the living room.

"Good morning," I sang. "Do you want me to fix you something?"

In an almost manic state, I raced to the kitchen to make us breakfast. After we ate, I stood up and started to clear the dishes from the table.

"Man, Meri," Eugene said. "What's going on with you? Why have you been drinking so much?"

I blew out a short breath and sniffed slightly to see whether I could smell alcohol on my breath. Sure enough, I smelled like a distillery.

"I don't know," I said. I plopped myself back onto the chair and announced, rather dramatically, "I think I am an alcoholic. I can't stop drinking. It's like a physical craving. Like I'm thirsty, except nothing else can quench it but liquor."

"When did you start drinking like that?" he asked.

"I don't remember. Three, maybe four months ago."

Eugene, refusing to accept that I was an alcoholic, came up with a probable explanation: Zoloft. I had been taking the drug for the same length of time.

"Stop taking it," he advised. "That's one way to find out if it's the cause of your drinking."

"If I stop taking my medicine, I'll get depressed again," I

complained. "Christmas is in a few weeks. I don't want to be depressed."

"Drinking will get you depressed again," he countered.

"I'll call my shrink and ask him whether I can stop."

"*Ask*?" he snapped. "You'd better call that man and *tell* him you need to stop. Why do you give people so much power over you? That M.D. behind his name just means that he's trained to facilitate your healing. You're the one who's actually got to make it happen. Therapy doesn't work unless you know what you want out of it. You're the one who has the power to change things."

The firmness in his voice startled me. Eugene had always pushed hard and been somewhat of a bully. That approach could easily have shattered another person, but it worked well with me since I'm stubborn. However, this determination seemed to be coming from some other place. He was displaying a level of personal investment in my wellness that I had never noticed before. Certainly I had always felt that he cared, but all the prior lectures and advice he gave me came from a place of friendship and love, a place that was close to yet also somehow removed from his heart. This time, he was speaking from a place of personal pain. Pure pain; the kind that grows out of helplessness, out of looking on as someone you care about deteriorates.

As soon as I stopped taking the Zoloft, I stopped drinking. It took a couple of weeks for the medicine to wear out of my system, but once it did, the desire to drink was completely gone. I don't know why the Zoloft affected me so adversely, that is, if it really did. I have often considered the possibility that maybe I was not ready to not be depressed, that maybe as much as I hated my moods, I had come to rely on them. They were the legs with which I had learned to walk. The alcohol, I suppose, was my crutch.

Antidepressants, Dr. Fitzgerald explained, are like any other medication—one brand does not suit all. He urged me to try out another medication to see if I would get better results than I had with the Zoloft. Since my initial venture into the world of psychopharmacology had gone awry, I was unenthusiastic about making a second one. If anything, I used my Zoloft ordeal to dismiss the probability that there was a medication out there that might very well work for me. Like the proverbial little engine that could, I went back once more to believing that I could kick this thing by myself.

Many depressives resist and refuse medication in hopes that they can "cure" themselves. I learned this when, after an unsuccessful go at it, I staggered back into Dr. Fitzgerald's office and begged for help. A big obstacle, he told me, in treating a diagnosed depression is not the illness itself, but the patient's reluctance to take medication.

At first, the depression that followed my detox from alcohol and Zoloft was not severe. There were no major episodes, only regular ups and downs, which, in and of themselves, were a sort of low-grade depression; but, overall, I felt sturdy and secure in my emotions. I made it through the holiday season, which has always been a hard time for me.

After emerging from a prolonged period of inertia and incapacity, one tends to want to make up for lost time. There is something that needs to be proved, to oneself and the entire world. It's an integral part of the cycle of depression. You do as much as you can, fill in as many gaps as possible until you crash and burn. Working as a writing instructor was ideal because of the amount of free time that I had. Time that, theoretically, I was supposed to be using for my own writing. In reality, that time was spent being preoccupied with how I was going to pay my bills.

I ended up taking another full-time position in addition to, not in place of, my part-time teaching job. I also founded a monthly reading series at the Los Angeles County Museum of Art. This was all within the first two months of 1994. It was far more activity and responsibility than I could handle. Illness, the next phase of the cycle, took over.

Dr. Fitzgerald put me on 20 milligrams of Prozac—which seemed to do the trick—and he also agreed to be my regular therapist. I wasn't thrilled about having a male therapist, but it was better than talking to someone with whom I was not familiar. We talked a lot about my day-to-day problems, but sometimes we also delved into my past and touched on issues of abandonment, sexual abuse, and my overall feelings of failure and worthlessness—all things, he claimed (and I reluctantly agreed), fed into my depression.

Each week, sometimes twice a week, I went to Dr. Fitzgerald's office. He was young, vibrant, kind; I liked him. It was obvious from our sessions that he genuinely cared about me and my progress, but the more I delved into my personal history, I got the sense that Dr. Fitzgerald was having a hard time understanding where I was coming from. This suspicion was cemented when I told him about a racial incident that occurred the day before a session. As far as racial incidents go, it was a rather common one.

I had gone into a store to return a dress. The clerk followed me as I walked throughout the store looking for another dress to buy with the credit I assumed I would be given for my return. Although she eyed me like a hawk, the clerk never asked if I needed help. In line, I stood behind a young white male also making a return, a gift that he wasn't even sure was purchased from that store. After hearing how kind and accommodating the cashier had been with him, I was appalled by the rudeness and suspicion with which she greeted me. She requested that I provide a receipt *and* personal identification. She badgered me with questions: "Are you sure you bought it here?"; "Have you already worn it?", none of which she had asked the previous customer.

Dr. Fitzgerald listened to my story. When I was through, he pushed out a breath of relief. "Whew," he said. "It must be so hard to be black. I can't even fathom having to contend with what you must deal with on a daily basis." For twenty minutes of my fifty-minute session, he talked about how he, as a white man, had never experienced prejudice in the same way that I probably had—as if I didn't already know this—but that he did sympathize with the hurt that incident must have caused me, blah, blah, blah.

I did not feel like Dr. Fitzgerald was patronizing me. In

fact, I was grateful for his honesty, problematic as it was. But if he was having a difficult time understanding the overt issues of my life—like racism—was there any way that he could be grasping the subtle ones? Racism is definitely in the eye of the beholder. White people have at hand the privilege of choosing whether to see or not see the racism that takes place around them. If Dr. Fitzgerald could not "fathom" my reality as a black person, how would he be able to assess or address the rage, the fear, and the host of other complex emotions that go hand-in-hand with being black in a racist society? For whatever reasons, seeing a black therapist had never crossed my mind, until then.

I do not believe that white therapists are unable to successfully treat people of color; however, I do think that they should possess a certain level of cultural sensitivity, as that culture plays an important role in both the patient's illness and treatment. I am black; I am female; I am an immigrant. Every one of these labels plays an equally significant part in my perception of myself and the world around me. If I am expected to investigate the events of my life with my therapist, then I expect him/her to have a working, if not fundamental, knowledge of how what I have lived factors into who I am and the ways in which I cope. A knowledge, preferably, that I do not have to give him/her myself.

With Shelly, I was completely at ease presenting the problems I faced trying to embrace two cultures and sort out how that process has affected my familial relationships. She did more than empathize with me; as a foreigner herself, she knew firsthand of what I spoke. Discussing my past sexual abuse and my inclination toward violent men was far more comfortable with Shelly than with Dr. Fitzgerald. Before we reached a place in our therapy sessions where race was presented as an issue, Shelly left, so I am not certain how or what I would have felt. There was much that I wanted to know about Dr. Fitzgerald but, because of what he kept insisting were professional confines, was not able to find out.

The point at which I became aware of Dr. Fitzgerald's possible limitations was when I followed Eugene's advice and took control of my own healing. Eugene was right; it is wise to be specific and certain about what it is that you wish to gain from therapy. Despite the reservations I had about Dr. Fitzgerald, I did not stop seeing him. Finding a new caregiver would have disrupted the strides I was making. Finally, I was releasing things that had been bottled up for years. I decided that what was most critical at this stage was for me to keep speaking, to continue being present in my life, past and present. Therapy was a safe place to do that.

It did not make that much of a difference to me if Dr. Fitzgerald was listening or not, if he cared or not, if he understood or not. *I* was listening. *I* was hearing. *I* was understanding. *I* cared. When the time came that I wanted more from a therapist than what Dr. Fitzgerald could offer, I would know enough to act accordingly.

———◆———

IN MARCH, Jade came to Los Angeles to visit her cousin, Aaron. She called me and asked if I could spend the day with her. We hadn't spoken since the time I called her at the hospital. I knew that she was doing remarkably well. She had been discharged after a two-week stay. Paula, whom I spoke with frequently, kept me up to date on Jade's progress. The two of them had become good friends.

I picked Jade up in the late morning and we drove toward the beach, with the windows rolled down, savoring the California sun. We were planning on going to Venice Beach for sushi and a stroll along the boardwalk. There were a number of things that each of us wanted to bring the other up to speed on. We made a pact to not get into the topic of depression until much later in the day, after our outing. We both just wanted to get away, laugh, and forget for a while that our lives are often fogged with despair.

We used surface roads to get to Venice Beach because the freeway had collapsed during the earthquake a couple of months back. It was a long ride from Silverlake, where Aaron stayed, to Venice. I made it even lengthier by taking the scenic route so that Jade and I could sightsee. She popped a cassette of Sade's *Love Deluxe* into the player. Our singing was interspersed with jokes and random commentaries about the people and houses that we drove by. When the song "Like a Tattoo" came on, Jade turned the volume up.

"Listen," she said. "Listen to these words."

I stopped talking and took in the lyrics. Jade turned the volume a notch higher and shook her head to the rhythm, "Right here." Still holding the knob, she sang along forcefully with a line, *"he spoke of his dreams . . . broken by the burden of his youth"*; then she turned to me and said,

"You know, I feel the same way. Like my dreams were broken by the burden of my youth, my depression. I don't even know if I dream anymore. I just try to not be depressed."

We never made it to the boardwalk. We sat in the restaurant for hours talking about the very topic we were trying to avoid, depression. She described what it was like to be in a mental institution. Therapy every day, several times a day; tests; observations; medication; isolation.

"They took the book that I was reading away from me," she complained.

"Why?" I demanded.

"My doctor didn't think it was a suitable piece of literature for 'someone like me'."

"What?" I asked in indignant wonder. "What was that all about? I would think they would have wanted you to read. Reading is supposed to be therapeutic. It's supposed to—" And then I remembered who I was talking to. Knowing Jade, it probably was an inappropriate book. "What were you reading?"

"*The Bell Jar,*" she said deviously. We both laughed. Only Jade would take a Sylvia Plath book with her to the psych ward. While she was there, Jade overcame her suicidal ideation and found a reason to fight. During one of her many physical examinations, she had seen her heart on an echocardiogram.

"I was one of the youngest patients there," she explained. "I guess the doctors were used to seeing old, battered organs. When the projection of my heart came up on the screen, one doctor told his assistant, 'Look at that. It's beautiful. It's perfect.' So I looked, too, and there was my heart. We always talk about our hearts, but how often do we get a chance to see them? All I could think of was the blood that was passing through it. The veins, the arteries, the vessels. That was what was keeping me alive; my heart. The doctor saw so much beauty and perfection in it, I thought that maybe if I stayed alive, I would eventually see it, too."

"This from a person who claims to not have dreams?" I teased. "I may not be able to see your heart, but I can sure see your face, and it's telling me that you are full of dreams."

"Maybe. I do have the same dreams I have always had. I said that they were broken by the burden of my depression. And that, I really do believe with all my heart."

The conversation that Jade and I had about dreams stayed on my mind for weeks. I thought about the real dreams that I had been having throughout the course of my battles with depression. Be it in flames or in water, I was always drowning in my dreams, being swallowed, being smothered by forces of nature while the people standing nearby watched as I suffered and struggled to stay alive. I wasn't sure what that meant. I got to wondering about my other dreams, the aspirations in my soul, not in my head. There were two, both of which involved the process of creation.

My strongest yearning was to build a career as a writer. The articles, the poems, and the stories that I had written were a start, but for twelve years I had been starting and never quite making it anywhere. In the beginning, when

I was younger, being a writer was a conceivable ambition; there was little doubt in my mind that I would make my living that way. The scales shifted somewhere along the line and the doubts began to outweigh the desire.

Korama ruled the other aspiration. Like the fiercest of poems, she was conceived when I least expected or appreciated the power that her presence would hold. I didn't know I had it in me to deliver something so beautiful to the world. But she was not a poem; she was a novel, a narrative that was unfolding day by day, page by page. As the person who was chosen to facilitate her development, I wanted to learn how to trust my instincts; I wanted to know when to utilize my skill and when to let go so her story could write itself. Simply put, I wanted to honor the person that she was by being a positive force in her life.

Like Jade, I felt that my dreams had gotten trapped under the stress of depression. They were definitely chipped and fractured in spots, but they were not broken. Even if they were, I believed that as long as I was alive, the damage was not irreparable. So I decided to go about the business of making them come true. That was all there was to it. That was the day, the first time ever in my life, that I made a commitment to being alive. Not the first time that I said that I wanted to live, or dreamed about living; it was the first time that I made a *commitment*, that I gave myself my word.

There was no master plan, no bolt of lightning from the sky, no cryptic calling. I was sick and tired of waiting for miracles, waiting for approval, waiting for happiness. For years I had been waiting, asking over and over and over and over, "Why me?" and I never found the answer so I figured what the hell, and decided to try asking, "Why not me?"

The pressure of working two jobs and wearing so many hats finally took its toll. I was becoming less and less productive at everything I was doing. There never seemed to be enough hours in the day. I was tired of constantly feeling like I was behind the eight-ball. Because of the change in my sleeping habits, I thought for sure that an episode of depression was on the horizon. I quit my day job. When I slowed my pace, I saw that it was not depression after all, just plain, old exhaustion, from having spread myself too thin.

One less job meant one less paycheck so I had to cut back on my spending. I made a list of my expenditures and, after careful deliberation, selected therapy as one of the things I could do without for a while. I was nearly twenty-seven years old. Every major detail of my life had been placed on the table. All the cards were face up. It had all been said, and resaid. And said again. I was sick of talking about the past. Moreover, it seemed self-defeating to spend the next twenty-seven years of my life hanging on to the pain of the first twenty-seven. Dr. Fitzgerald thought I was being drastic.

"For someone who wanted to take their time learning how to walk, you're being a tad hasty about getting out there and trying to fly, don't you think?"

I recognized his concern. I had heard those words, or

some variation of them, a thousand times. Ordinarily, I would have gotten defensive. I would have tried to get him to agree, or at least see, that I was right and he was wrong, but I wasn't feeling it that day. I didn't care if he was right.

Ending that particular round of therapy turned out to be a wise decision. It afforded me the opportunity to shift my consciousness, and the distance to digest everything that I had taken in. It was not, by any stretch of the imagination, my last encounter with psychotherapy. When I was ready, I began a new relationship with a new therapist, and worked with her until I felt that I had gone as far as I could go in her care. It has been refreshing and, ultimately, transformative to work with different people. Though I have not yet found a therapist whom I feel is 100% "right" for me, each one that I have worked with—there have been six in total—has brought me a little closer to being well and, to borrow a phrase from the pop psychology books, "fully realized."

——◆——

I SCHEDULED A trip to D.C. to visit with family and friends. In the back of my mind, I was also hoping to drum up some more writing assignments. In the last hour of the flight, I had a massive fit of anxiety. Korama and I were going to be staying with my mother. After spending so much time talking about her in therapy, I was terrified to lay eyes on her. I figured that she was going to give me grief about my dreads, which she never failed to inform me were not very Ghanaian.

Korama and I took the Metro from the airport. Mum picked us up from the subway station. I put Korama in the back and strapped her into the carseat that Mum kept for our visits. I offered my mother a weak smile as I slid into the passenger seat and then turned my eyes and my entire upper body toward the window.

"Nana-Ama, let me look at your face," she requested. I took a deep breath, turned my head in her direction, and waited to hear what she had to say. "Look at your hair. It makes you look like, like, like, you know."

"I don't know what you're talking about," I said coldly. I turned my head back toward the window and she started driving.

"You know you were really plump when you were a baby," she continued. It figures, I thought to myself, she's telling me that I'm fat. She always seemed to zero in on my biggest insecurity. "We used to call you Ma'am B," she kept on. "Everybody who saw you would squeeze your cheeks because they were so cute. When you were growing up, you were so thin. You lost those puffy cheeks. But your hair. Now that it's longer, it softens your face, makes your cheeks rounder. You look nice."

It was actually a very sweet thing for her to say because I knew that she had initially hated the idea of me locking my hair, but I was too upset from the anticipation of negativity.

"Oh," I muttered, keeping my eyes fixed on the window.

When we entered The Ivy, Jade and Paula were sitting on the stoop, waiting for us. I jumped out of the car before my mother could place the gear in park, leaving her to tend to Korama, without so little as a thank you for the ride.

The next day while Paula was at school and Mum was at work, I started cleaning up the toys that Korama had left lying around the living room. At the far end of the couch, I could see the toes of a baby-doll leg sticking out from one of the corners. As I got on all fours to pull it out, I discovered a photo album. I pulled both the doll and the album out from under the couch, then sat down to look at what I thought would be old family photos.

Inside the album was every article that had ever been written about me, every performance program from the shows I had produced, flyers from poetry readings I forgot I had even participated in. It was a record of my entire career as an artist. I was blown away. All along while I was sending my mother reviews, articles, poems, trying to get some praise or encouragement, she was keeping a scrapbook!?

Finding the scrapbook and seeing all my past accomplishments made me feel wonderful; it motivated me to call my editor at the *Post*. I asked him if we could get together for lunch the next day but, he said, Fridays were bad for him.

"I can do it early next week," he offered.

I was only in town through that Monday. Monica, Jade's sister, had offered to babysit for me on Friday so that I could run errands. My flight was leaving in the early evening on Monday and I wasn't sure if I could squeeze in a trip to the city and make it back to The Ivy in time. And even if I could, I didn't know if Monica or Jade would be able to watch Korama.

"I'm leaving on Monday," I told him. "But I wanted to know if I could run an article idea by you."

"Sure," he responded. "We can always use something good. What do you have in mind?"

I couldn't think of any of the query ideas I had come up with while I was still in L.A. I tossed the first idea that popped into my head, something about the black church and homosexuality. He asked me what my angle was and, of course, I didn't have one.

"Think of one," he advised. "And call me back. By the way, what've you been up to? I haven't heard from you in a while."

"You don't even want to know," I laughed. In what ended up being an extremely long-winded anecdote, I told him all about my bouts with depression, the Zoloft, the drinking, the therapy, the Prozac. Just like in the conversation we had about my job as a phone sex operator, the more questions he asked, the more I revealed.

"There's your story right there," he said.

"Not a chance in hell," I responded.

"That's the same thing you said about the phone sex piece and look how popular that was. There's a whole lot of stuff being written about depression these days. Have you read William Styron's book? If you were to write a piece, you'd have to make sure that you weren't repeating what's already been said, which will be pretty hard to do."

"Yeah, right," I said sarcastically. "Like Styron and I would ever have the same angle on anything. We had the same illness; the similarities end there. The way I did depression was a-whole-nother bag of beans. I'm a single black mother about a half a paycheck away from the government cheese line."

"There you have it," he said, as if he'd struck gold. "Make it about two thousand words, no more than twenty-five hundred. You can keep it personal, but you've gotta hook into what's going on out there. Remember to push the transcendence key. I've gotta run to a meeting. Call me if you get stuck. Bye."

And then he hung up. I tried to call him back and tell him that I didn't want to write the piece, but his voice mail picked up, and I didn't leave a message.

When Paula got home from school, she and I sat down and talked about her therapy. We also exchanged horror stories about our experiences with Zoloft. She had stopped taking the medication because she claimed that she didn't feel "normal" under its influence. I asked her to define normal.

"I can't," she said. "But I know it doesn't come in a pill."

Paula had also stopped going to therapy. The therapist she was seeing moved on to private practice and Paula did not want to continue her sessions with a new therapist.

"What are you going to do now?" I asked her.

"I don't know. What are you going to do?"

"I don't know," I said.

We were both at a crossroads. I had a feeling that she, like I, did know what she was going to do to fill her chasms, but it was not something that could be easily articulated. Paula is in college now and, like most young adults, I suppose she is trying to "find" herself. To the best of my knowledge, she never resumed medication or went back into therapy. I don't know why because she never told me. She does not volunteer much, if any, information about herself. Asking feels too much like prying, so I don't. Our relationship is evolving, although right now, I can't tell exactly how, or into what.

After Paula and I had talked about therapy, I pulled out the album I found earlier.

"What's this all about?" I asked, handing it to her. She flipped through the first few pages.

"You've never seen it before?"

"No," I said. "It was under the couch."

"It must have fallen. It's normally there, next to the lamp." She was pointing to the end table in the living room. "Mommy shows it to everybody who comes over and she brags about her daughter, the writer."

I stayed up most of the night thinking about whether or not to write the article on depression. The word "suffering" kept coming to mind. That, to me, was what depression was all about, suffering. I looked up the definition of the word in order to grasp its full meaning. To suffer is to feel pain, to sustain an unbearable condition; it is also to be disadvantaged. Ignorance then is a kind of suffering; fear is a kind of suffering. Before my depression was diagnosed, I had suffered at the hands of ignorance and fear. I never wanted to feel that way again. I never wanted to be deprived of knowledge that could be beneficial to my well-being. If I could help alleviate anyone else's suffering by writing the article, then I wanted to do it.

The next morning, I called Mrs. Bledsoe and asked her

if I could drop by. She was warm and receptive. We made plans to get together at her house the following day for tea and a chat. Somewhere in the back of my mind, I think I was searching for a mother figure. I wanted to talk to someone who could help me find the words I had been searching for, the ones I needed to bridge the gap between me and my own mother.

———◆———

WHILE MRS. BLEDSOE was in the kitchen preparing tea for our visit, I wandered through the first floor of her house, museum-style, with my hands clasped behind my back, looking at the pictures, wood carvings, and assorted curios. Her home was immaculate and magnificently decorated. I was sure that there was a story behind each book, painting, and quilt. Years' worth of stories. Years' worth of travels and memories. I wanted to hear each one; I wanted to know who the people in all the photographs were, what they were doing, thinking, feeling. Most of them were of the Bledsoe family, embracing, smiling. Except for one in the kitchen, that one was of Patricia, alone. She looked introspective, as if someone had snuck up on her and taken the picture while she was deep in thought.

"That was taken in 1972," Mrs. Bledsoe said, looking over my shoulder.

"It's beautiful," I said, tracing the edges of the frame with my fingers. Mrs. Bledsoe acknowledged the compliment with a quick smile as she put two cups of hot tea and a plate of sandwiches down on the small, circular kitchen table.

"Eugene has told me a lot about you," I said, moving toward the table and then sitting down.

"Oh he has, has he?" she replied, taking a seat. She didn't sound upset or even curious. She had a pretty good idea of what I was leading up to. I had already told her in our phone conversation that I wanted to talk to her about depression. Mentioning Eugene was simply a polite formality, a way to ease into the subject.

"He told me about when you first started getting depressed," I proceeded, "and about how hard it was for you to find out what was wrong with you."

"I'll tell you," she said, shaking her head, "that was something else. I don't know if 'hard' is the right word. Eugene was so young then. I still wonder how that affected him, not having his mother around during that time. When I was there, I wasn't really *there*."

She retreated into a pensive silence, the same kind she was probably in when that photograph was taken. "How's the baby?" she finally asked.

"Korama's fine," I answered. "She's three years old now. Talking, walking, and being all grown."

"Take it in while you can," she advised. "It goes by fast. Too fast."

I used the discussion of Korama to redirect the conversation back to depression.

"I've always been a melancholy person," I told her. "But after I had Korama, it just went to another level. It was one episode of depression on top of another. I couldn't tell where one ended and another one began. I don't know, maybe something physical happened to me during the pregnancy and childbirth. I developed toxemia while I was carrying, but . . . I don't know, maybe it wasn't that. Maybe I was just overwhelmed by everything that happened in my life after I had her."

"It's possible that your pregnancy triggered something," she said. "A month after I had Robert, my youngest, I had a stroke. I don't know if Eugene mentioned it, but that's when I first started going through these depressions."

When Eugene told me about his mother's battle with depression, he had only given me a skeleton of facts about how she found out she was depressed, how often her depression came, and the various treatments she tried. Mrs. Bledsoe fleshed out that skeleton by inserting the specifics—what, when, where, and why. Most of our conversation about the first eight years of her depression, I have already incorporated into an earlier segment of this book. I was also very interested in who and how she was before she had the stroke. At my request, Mrs. Bledsoe went backwards in her life and told me about her childhood and adolescence.

"I was born in Georgia, in a small town right outside of Atlanta. It was old and dusty and rural. I lived with my mother, my father, and my younger brother. We had a regular family life. But, when I was three years old, my mother ran away with another man. He was an older man, a deacon at a Baptist church—"

"Your mother just up and left you guys?" I asked in disbelief.

"Yep. She was young, about twenty-two years old. My father was a couple of years older. She met this man, Ray, at a regional conference of the Baptist Church Association. After she disappeared with Ray, I didn't see her again for a few years. They went to Atlanta, although we didn't find that out until later. When Mom first left, none of us knew where she was, not even my father."

I had heard plenty about fathers leaving their families, but this was the first I'd ever heard about a mother doing something like that. Somehow I'd always imagined that mothers were genetically programmed to be the nurturing ones, the ones who stayed forever, despite whatever.

"Why did your mother do that?" I asked her.

"She was a flamboyant woman in her youth. I think she must have felt trapped in that tiny town with her tiny family, teaching at a tiny little country day school. All that smallness probably couldn't hold the size of her attention. She wanted to be in the big city, where the action was, so she took the chance when it came her way."

"What did your dad do after she left him?"

"We—my father, brother, and I—went to live with my great-aunt, Mama Linda. Mama Linda took us in and raised my brother and me for a few years. Back then, the whole experience of having, and sometimes living with, an extended family was rather common. We had a rich community life and as a result, I wasn't all that lonely." I found it hard to believe that she wasn't lonely, even with all that family around. Nobody can replace a mother.

"You didn't miss your mother at all?"

"Yes. Sometimes. I was really young, four or five at the time, but I clearly remember feeling the emotional deprivation of losing my mother. I remember sitting in the dirt behind the old schoolhouse one day. My face was buried in my knees and I was sobbing so hard I could feel the drops of tears trickling down the sides of my legs. Charlie-Ann Hackenberry, this girl that lived down the way, came up and asked me why I was crying. 'I miss my mother,' I told her, 'I miss her so much.'

"And then, shortly after that day, an uncle of mine who lived in Atlanta spotted my mother."

"Did she come back home to you guys?" I asked, my heart aching for the motherless child that Mrs. Bledsoe once was.

"No. I can't recall how long a period of time it was from when he saw her until we heard from her again, but she did slowly start to reestablish contact. She sent me care packages. That went on for a while and then she came for me when I was in the third grade. I don't know why, but I was the only one who went to the city with her. My brother never left Mama Linda's. That was his home until he reached manhood."

"Were she and that man still together?"

"Yes. She eventually left him, but I don't know why. Mom had a lot of husbands and boyfriends. She was married five times, every other year it seemed like. It got to be a little embarrassing because each time she got remarried, we had a new last name. I hated my mother."

"Well," I shrugged, "it seems only natural to dislike your mother after what she did to you."

"No, Meri. I mean I really hated her, until well after I was a mother myself. Running out on us was only the beginning. She was extremely unpleasant to me, and that's putting it mildly. The truth is that she was downright mean. I don't remember ever being hugged or kissed by her throughout my entire childhood. She never let me have company or talk on the phone. That made living at home feel like being in prison because I had no one to spend time with."

Imagining Mrs. Bledsoe growing up with such cruelty brought tears to my eyes. She started to cry, too.

"She neglected my needs to fulfill her own. She was really pretty, like the fashion models in the magazines, and she dressed real well. All the new clothes that she bought were for her. She hardly ever bought me anything new or nice to wear. I don't want to give you the impression that I was wearing rags to school, but let's just say it was obvious, at a glance, that the other kids in school were better taken care of than me. I always wondered why she came for me if she didn't really want to have me around."

"Did you have any friends?" I asked.

"Oh, lots. I did well in school. I guess you could say that I was popular. When I was in the twelfth grade, I was a drum major, one of those girls that marches in front of the band during parades. I was dating the captain of the football team. He was a handsome fellow, but when it came down to it, we didn't have very much in common. He and I got married when I was seventeen because I was pregnant with my daughter, Laura. I was pregnant when I started college, and Laura was born in January of 1949, midway through my first year. While she was still an infant, I left her father because he was physically abusive. Laura and I went to live with Mama Linda. By the time I was nineteen, I was divorced. Luckily, I was able to re-enroll in college. That's where I met Gilbert, my present husband.

"Gilbert's sister, who was my friend, went to the same college. Gilbert and I started dating, but then he was drafted during the Korean War. While he was away, I moved to Lansing. After he returned, he finished college and moved up to Detroit, Michigan, to live with his uncle and look for work. We started dating again. He got a job in Lansing and then, a year later, in 1955, he and I were married. Eugene was born in 1958. Right about then, my mother was living in Louisville, Kentucky. After the children were born, she tried to be kind to me, but I wouldn't let her. I did keep in contact with her, and we visited her from time to time, for the children's sake. She came to Lansing once to visit us and she liked it so much that she moved there. She met and married her last husband there. They were together for over twenty years. I had my last child, Robert, in 1960. Exactly one month, to the day, after Robert was born, I had the stroke. You pretty much already know what happened after that."

"Just up to the time when Dr. Thorpe put you on the Elavil and started giving you outpatient shock treatments. But, obviously, your episodes of depression didn't stop for good."

"That treatment worked for about four or five years. I wasn't in psychotherapy then. I was just taking the medicine and getting the shock treatments. I suppose the Elavil served its purpose, but the shock treatments were more effective."

"When did you start seeing a therapist?"

"In 1969, we moved to Washington, D.C. I was depressed that entire year. It was the first time I had been depressed through the spring and summer as well. I started seeing this psychotherapist, Frank Priggam, who didn't buy into this whole business of medication and shock therapy. But seeing him was helpful. He brought me to my first level of understanding about my mother."

"Were you and your mother still in contact?"

"Every few months, Gil and I would take the kids to Lansing to see her. Just knowing that I would have to hug her, to touch her, made me sick to my stomach. And as great as Dr. Priggam was, the depression persisted and eventually became unbearable. I convinced him to admit me into the Washington Hospital Center for shock treatment."

I interrupted Mrs. Bledsoe.

"How does shock treatment feel? This probably sounds stupid, but does it hurt?"

"The doctors give you this anesthesia, it's like a muscle relaxant. You can feel it flowing through your body. It starts from the tip of your toes and then tingles its way up through the rest of you. By the time it hits your midsection, you are completely under, or at least, you should be.

"Something went wrong with my last treatment. The doctors were to be administering treatment to both sides of my brain. I was not fully asleep when the electricity passed through me. It wasn't pain that I felt. It was definitely shock, like sticking not just one, but all ten of your fingers into an electrical socket. That was the worst possible feeling to live through. You'd better believe it was the last time I received shock therapy. I'll be the first to admit that, for me, it works better than anything else, but I'd rather go without it than risk feeling what I felt ever again, even if the possibility is remote.

"I stayed in the hospital for several weeks. After I was released, I went back into therapy with Dr. Priggam. He and I worked together until he retired the next year. After Dr. Priggam, I had therapy with a black woman psychiatrist, Dr. Myrtle Summit, for six years. We worked on my relationship with my mother and I was finally able to make peace with her. I actually learned to love her. I learned to hold her before she died. About seven or eight years before she passed, she wrote me a letter. She had been diagnosed with cancer, but she chose to keep it a secret from us until she was close to dying. I read the letter and put it away for a number of years. In the letter, she wrote that she was aware of how badly she had treated me when I was younger. She asked for my forgiveness because, she said, she was young then and did not know any better."

"She didn't know any better?" I repeated sarcastically. Just hearing about the pain Mrs. Bledsoe had been through made me feel very protective of her.

"Had I not had children myself, it would have been difficult for me to understand how someone could not have known any better than to be so emotionally cruel to her own child. Having been a young mother myself, I understand what she meant by that. You grow to know life's complexities. Good, bad, or indifferent, all mothers leave their children with a lot to be desired. That's because we're all tackling life at the same time that we're trying to raise and do right by our children. I realized that my mother was a young woman. She was still trying to get hers from the world. I eventually wrote her back and told her that I had forgiven her, that I did understand and that I did love her, very much. In fact, I was right by her side when she died."

This made me think about Korama. As she got older, what would her thoughts be on my mothering? Would this illness block her vision of my attempts to do right by her? Would she see it as an illness, or assume it was just part of my character, and allow it to negatively define our relationship? I didn't want my depression to be the only thing that defined or distinguished me and my life. This was something I wanted to work on, by myself and in therapy.

"Do you still see a therapist?" I asked Mrs. Bledsoe.

"No," she replied. "As far as I'm concerned, there comes a point where therapy is no longer useful. I felt very healthy emotionally. All the quote-unquote problem areas of my life had been worked out and every winter, I still got depressed. There are all sorts of reasons why people get depressed and stay depressed. But depression, in its most basic, clinical form, is biochemical. It is an illness. Some people get through it and it never returns. For thirty-seven years, my depression has returned nearly every winter. I have reconciled myself with the fact that I am going to have to deal with this for the rest of my life.

"In my case, I feel that medication is the only thing that will work. Right now I see a psychopharmacologist who is based at the National Institutes of Mental Health. I go to him and we try out different drugs. It's a process of trial and error. Some of the medications I have taken are fine one year and then cease to be effective the next, and then the depression returns. Right now I am taking a drug called Pamelor. It worked very well through this last cycle of depression. I'm just hoping that come September, it'll still be working."

Before leaving, I took one last look at that photograph, the one of just her. There was a haunting feeling to it. I silently guessed that she was going through a depression when the picture was taken. It was not so much the look that she had on her face, but the one that was shining through from underneath.

"It's funny," she said, reading my mind. "People who know, can tell immediately. My daughter, Laura, can always tell. She can hear it in my voice, even when I am trying to disguise it. The instant she saw that photograph, she said, 'Mom, you were depressed then.'"

"Thank God that Korama's too young to know," I said.

"She's too young to tell you," Mrs. Bledsoe corrected. "But she's not too young to know."

The INFINITE POWER of CHANGE

what hurt me so terribly
all my life until this moment?
How I love the small, swiftly
beating heart of the bird
singing in the great maples;
its bright, unequivocal eye

—Jane Kenyon

from "Having It Out with Melancholy"

I USED TO think that change was a negative thing. My life had been so marred by it. Change equaled loss, and loss meant grief. I have spent the better part of my life dwelling on the past instead of facing the future. I have spent more than my share of time drenched in sorrow, feeling rejected and lonely.

Usually, I don't care much for the company of others, but when I was depressed, I used to hate being alone because I felt as though I stopped existing when I was by myself. In a continual effort to stay attuned to the world around me, I clung to whomever was closest. I entered relationships solely to veil my insatiable need for companionship, for a life support system. I know that I demanded the impossible from people. Perhaps I even demanded too much from life. When my life started to feel as though it were slipping from my hands, my instant inclination was to scream, to cry out for help from anyone who could hear me; but that meant I would run the risk of destroying my facade of adult sensibility, of strength, so instead of exploding, I would implode; that collapse, inevitably, brought about a depression.

This is one of the reasons I have come up with to explain how my episodes of depression are triggered. There are others—many, many others. When I returned from that last trip to Washington, D.C., I sat down and made a list of them. I thought that if I could not change the fact that I have a tendency toward depression, I could at least manipulate the circumstances that cause these depressions. With the help of the first list, I created another one, a list of precautions, ways in which I could prevent myself from falling into a depression. I noticed, for instance, that besides my daughter and myself, there were no living things in my home. There were no fish, no birds, no cats or dogs. I went out and bought plants because I thought that they would be easy to take care of. They all died. I bought more. Those died, too. One after the other, I kept bringing plants into my home until, at last, I learned how to tend to them. That was a major coup. It probably sounds ridiculous, but I saw my plants as an extension of myself. If they thrived, I thrived, my daughter thrived.

After the plants came the music. Some people read daily affirmations or words of wisdom to get them on the right emotional track for the day. I chose music, one inspirational song, to accompany my meditative moment each morning. The other lifestyle alterations were added slowly and, sometimes, unintentionally. I began exercising every morning; I changed my diet. Once a week, Korama and I had a set "date"; we spent the day baking, going to the park, or the movies.

It was challenging for me to remain consistent with the strategies that I developed. I had never been able, before, to abide by schedules or plans. An impulsive person, I had always allowed my passions to guide me—in my writing, my mothering, my friendships. With the help of my present therapist, I am learning to find a balance, to distinguish between moods and passions that are healthy and beneficial and those that lead me into self-destructive situations.

I sometimes tend to focus more closely on my failures than on my successes. Not so long ago, whenever I strayed from my set routine, I beat myself up with guilt. Guilt, of course, is a key ingredient in the recipe for depression; it precedes punishment. The only remedy I could come up with for guilt was forgiveness. Letting go was not my style, not where my faults were concerned. I found that it was easier to forgive someone else their transgressions than it was to forgive myself for what I perceived were mine. Every night, before I went to bed, I said out loud, "I forgive myself for———," and then I would fill in the blank with whatever I had done or not done. This enabled me to leave the mistakes of each day in that day.

These techniques were important in helping me monitor my moods and deal with my stress, but they did not shield me from the outside world, where I could encounter any number of events that might set off a disastrous reaction. Social situations can be dangerous. They are like hidden land mines. I can be a grossly insecure person with an uncanny ability to shred compliments into insults; and then I use these perceived insults to tear apart my self-esteem. These days, I am doing this less and less. As the saying goes, I look and hear *with* strength, not *for* it. As my sense of self-worth has increased, the compulsion for self-deprecation has decreased.

When I look around me, it is difficult to imagine a time when I did not feel at ease in my skin, in my life. There is much for me to be proud of: I have an intelligent daughter who offers me the purest love I have ever known; my writing career, which I dreamed of and wished for, is becoming a reality. Despite all of this, I still experience episodes of depression—but they are different now. In comparison to the episodes that I experienced in the past, the ones I now have are infrequent, slight. And I do not suffer through them. I know that wherever I am standing, a healing force is right beside me and I surrender to that, not to the illness. I immediately go and get help. Generally, I can feel when a depression is coming on. It is no different than detecting the onset of any other illness. And, as with other illnesses, the earlier it is detected, the better one's chances are of not being debilitated by it.

Medical science has no cure for depression. Therapy and antidepressants are merely treatments. Despite current advancements in the treatment of depressive disorders, doctors still know very little about them. The supposed facts and statistics that are disseminated about depressive disorders are discouraging: the ratio of women to men that are diagnosed with depression is 2 to 1; over half of the people who have survived depression will most likely find themselves battling it again sometime down the line; depression is more common among first-degree blood relatives of people with the disorder.

Add to all this the social and economic realities of women, blacks, single parents, or any combination of the three, and my chances for a life that is free of depression appear to be slim. I, and others like me, seem to be doomed right from the get-go. While I recognize the importance of such information, I regard most of the data as blather and refuse to embrace it.

Personally, I choose to believe that somewhere, somehow, there is a cure for depression. I have to. But I think the healing, the reversal, must take place in the spirit, as well as the body. Therapy is crucial. Often I am asked whether the depressions I have are emotional or biochemical. Having posed that question myself a million times before, I am well aware of its implications, that an emotional depression is less profound, more topical because it is issue-related, and has very little to do with one's brain chemistry. As all our emotions and moods are biochemically induced, regardless of whether the prompts are internal or external, this supposition is false. All clinical depressions are a mixture of the emotional and the biochemical; the illness exists somewhere in that ghost space between consciousness and chemistry. That is why depressives who are on medication are encouraged, if not required, to also be in therapy.

Reluctantly, I am on medication. I take ten milligrams of Paxil a day. On a number of occasions while I have been in a depression, I have tried to deny my need for medication and stopped taking it. Each time, at the slightest provocation, I have fallen, fast and hard, deeper into the depression. Knowing the physical and psychological anguish that the illness can cause, I am all for whatever works—be it electroshock, antidepressant medication, or homeopathy. Still, there is something that seems really wrong with the fact that Prozac is one of the most prescribed drugs in this country. Maybe I just don't want to accept the reality that so many of us are in pain.

One Saturday a month, I host a meeting in my home for women of color. At these meetings, we sit for hours and entrust each other with our problems, our lives. When I first decided to start hosting these sessions, issues of trust and privacy weighed heavily on my mind. With my therapist, I knew that whatever I divulged remained in that room. Or at least, it was, by law, supposed to. With my friends and acquaintances, I did not have the same insurance.

What I discovered when I took my chances and revealed myself to these women was that nothing I was experiencing or had ever experienced was a deep, dark secret to them. We were all able to find common ground and individual courage in each other's testimonies. I learned that a large number of the black women whom I called colleagues and friends had battled or were still battling depression; it had crept into the most ostensibly perfect facades. Then why the silence and the stigma surrounding the subject? Why do we continue to allow one another to live with the shame and the secrecy of mental illness?

Last year, my friend, Scott Riley, fell ill with depression. In his eighth year of sobriety, Scott was no stranger to emotional hardship. He had carefully salvaged and then rebuilt his life from the ashes of addiction. After I relocated to Los Angeles, Scott and I talked about twice a month, sometimes less, but rarely more. In December of 1994, he began to call me more often. At first it was once or twice a week and then it was once or twice a day. I could tell right away that he was sinking into a depression. Whenever we spoke, he berated himself to me throughout the entire conversation.

In the time that I had known Scott, I had never heard him spout that much negativity about anything, let alone himself. He would call at eleven in the evening or at midnight, Pacific time, which meant that he was wide awake at two and three in the morning, Eastern time. The signs were all there—insomnia, self-loathing. I told him what I suspected and he readily agreed with me. In fact, he had already started going to therapy.

One of the most heart-felt admissions that Scott made to me at the onset of his illness was that although he had stood by me throughout various cycles of my depression, he had never really understood what it meant to be depressed.

"Depression," he told me, "is like a migraine. You can explain and describe the pain until you're blue in the face, but people have no point of reference to associate it with except what they have confronted. They assume that because they have had bad headaches, they can relate to your migraine, but they can't. Migraines aren't bad headaches, they're migraines. And depression isn't the same as ordinary sadness, it is hell."

I talked to Scott whenever he called and tried to help him through the depression by urging him to continue seeing his therapist and by telling him, as many times as he needed to hear it, that I felt he was worthy of life, of love, and of happiness. These reassurances sounded superficial to my ears, so I know that given the state he was in, they must have seemed stupid and dismissive. He stopped calling and, after two or three days, I phoned him to make sure he was alright but was unable to reach him. Four weeks later, he returned my call. He sounded calmer, more rational.

The change I heard in his voice was the progress of his therapy and the result of Anaphenol, tranquilizers, and a three-week stay at the psychiatric ward of a hospital. Scott had attempted suicide. The day after the last conversation he and I had, Scott had taken a bottle-full of Thyroxin, the medication prescribed for his dog's thyroid disease. The amount he took was lethal to humans, eight times over, and would have caused him to have a massive heart attack had he not walked to the hospital and admitted himself for treatment. I asked Scott what made him decide that he wanted to live after all.

"It wasn't a conscious change of heart," he confessed. "I put on my clothes and started walking to the hospital. I just left it up to fate. If I died before I got to the hospital then so be it; if I lived, then I would get some help and try to make it through. That's what I told myself then, but looking back, I see that I must have wanted to live all along. You know that I'm an alcoholic. My roommates drink. There was plenty of liquor in the house. If I had really wanted to die, I would have washed those pills down with a drink, but I didn't. I took them with a glass of apple juice."

While I was trying to help Scott through the initial phase of his depression, prior to his suicide attempt, I realized for the first time how painful it is to witness the way depression erodes people's will. With Jade and with Paula, I was ill at the same time that they were, so I incorporated the pain of their ordeals with my own. I would even go so far as to say that it was, in a way, reassuring to know that I could share my ordeal with someone who was going through a similar one.

With Scott, I felt powerless. His need was as deep and yawning as a cavern. There seemed to be very little I could do to fill it. Even though I knew it was impossible, I wanted to save him singlehandedly; I wanted to impart some knowledge to him, lend him a bit of optimism, anything to pull him out of the fog. Instead, I lectured more than I listened and I cried more than I consoled. In him I saw myself, and I hated that. I hated the feelings of helplessness that were sparked by the sound of his voice. Most of all, I hated knowing that not so long ago, I had been where Scott was and Eugene had been where I now was.

The article that I was to write on black women and depression was never published. I found that I had more to say and share on that topic than my assigned word count allowed. My editor at *The Washington Post* convinced me to write a book, so I did. As I neared the completion of my manuscript a friend, Ursula Mavis, asked what the book was going to be called.

"Willow Weep for Me," I told her. "Like the song."

That title, I thought, not only invoked Billie Holiday's image and the tragedy that was her life, it also called attention to the necessity of the long-overdue inclusion of black women in discussions about depression.

While writing, I started to rethink this title. It seemed to suggest that black women were victims. I wanted a title that would reflect the courage, devotion, and resilience that it takes to contend with depression. There is no other word besides resilience to describe what it must have taken Patricia Bledsoe to live with depression for thirty-seven years, what it took for Jade Parsons to see the splendor in her heart and the value of her life.

"That's amazing," Ursula replied when I told her the title. "I've been writing a lot of poetry lately about my own triumph over depression," she said. "I call it my 'Willow' series."

"That old weeping willow tree," I joked. "It's sure seen a lot of victims and a lot of tears."

"We're not victims, we're survivors. The willow is a healing herb," she told me. "One of the chemicals in the bark of the tree is the same ingredient that was originally used to make aspirin. Isn't that inspirational?"

Further research confirmed this information. The willow tree was once a symbol of joy. It grew along the banks of the

Nile River and the Hebrews admired and adopted the tree in their ceremonies because of its magnificence and grace. It was after the Jews' Babylonian exile that the willow tree began to represent the act of weeping, the mourning over loss, and the litany for survival. Psalm 137 describes the misery the Jews felt after being banished from their home: "By the rivers of Babylon, there we sat down, yea, we wept, when we remembered Zion; We hanged our harps upon the Willows in the midst thereof; For there they that carried us away captive required of us a song; and they that wasted us required of us mirth, saying, 'Sing us one of the songs of Zion.'"

The active chemical in the bark of the willow tree is salicin. It was used in the early 1800s to make salicylic acid, the precursor to aspirin. Another herb, meadowsweet, also contains salicin. Aspirin (acetylsalicylic acid) is made from the salicin that is obtained from meadowsweet. Indeed the willow is a symbol of healing.

About a month ago I was listening to my morning song, "Alive in the World," and preparing myself for my workout when Korama, who had been dressing herself for school, called me. I rushed right into her room to tend to her.

"What's up," I asked.

She pointed to the fish in the small bowl that was sitting atop her dresser. We had just bought four goldfish the week before. She named them Korama, Meri, Justin, and Paula—after the most significant people in her life. To me, they all pretty much looked alike, but she claimed to be able to tell them apart.

"Look," she said. "It's dying."

"That one's Justin, right?" I asked, drawing an imaginary line from her index finger to the fish she was pointing out.

"No," she insisted. "It's Meri."

I studied the fish closely and could not see what Korama meant. Meri, the goldfish, appeared to be swimming as effortlessly as the others. I tried to convince Korama that she was probably mistaken.

"Okay," she shrugged. "I hope you're right."

I drove Korama to school and spent an hour at the gym. When I returned home, I went into her room to tidy up. That's when I noticed what she had been trying to tell me. I glanced over at the bowl and realized that Meri's movement was not the same as the others. She was gliding in the center alongside her fellow fish, but it was obvious she was having a hard time keeping up. She was sluggish and listless. I watched her take the water into her gills, one slow gulp at a time. She was definitely dying. While my eyes followed the fish, I thought back to the times when I felt as if I was dying, trying my best to match the strides of the people around me. The fish eventually died; it floated to the surface and stayed there, like a leaf, flat and stationary. For a second, I thought I would cry until I realized I was actually very happy that it was not me who had been in distress.

But I was concerned for Korama. How will I explain this to her? I wondered. I found it troubling that my daughter was overly attuned to pernicious subtleties. She was too young to be so knowledgeable about death. What I wanted her to know was life. It troubled me that her lessons on suffering had been learned by watching her mother. I know how that feels. I watched my own mother suffer and I breathed in her misery, and all its staleness, like air.

There was a sadness, a sort of mournful resignation, to my mother that, as a child, I sensed but couldn't comprehend. Her eyes were always dimly lit. In the evenings of my youth, my mother would come home from work, prepare dinner for my sister and me but, no matter how early the hour, she would retire to her room. She spent the rest of the night in her bed behind closed doors. I often read to keep myself company. Sadness was as thick a bond between us as blood.

———————

CHANGE CONTINUES TO BE a major signifier for my life. Instead of focusing on what the changes take away, I find myself looking forward to what they will bring, how they will enhance. The past does not loom over me like an ax dangling from the thin strand of happenstance. It informs my present, but it does not weigh down my future. The more I change, the more I find that the people around me have changed. Maybe they really have, or maybe the only thing that has changed is my perception, the way I internalize and react to the world around me.

Before, I used to wonder what my life would have been like had I not gone through my depressions; now, I don't know if I would trade those experiences. I love who I am. And without those past depressions, I wouldn't be the same person. Through the depressions, through therapy, I have learned to speak out, to claim the life that I want, and to cherish the people with whom I choose to share it. Having lived with the pain, having felt/heard/seen and tasted it, I know now that when you pass through it, there is beauty on the other side.

AFTERWORD

Wouldn't Take Nothing for My Journey Now

———

Are you sure, sweetheart, that you want to be well? . . . Just so's you're sure, sweetheart, and ready to be healed, cause wholeness is no trifling matter. A lot of weight when you're well.

—Toni Cade Bambara, *The Salt Eaters*

THE BIGGEST STRUGGLE of my life has been with silence. It has been the umbrella under which all of my other challenges have sought shelter, a convenient place for them to hide, to grow, to fester. I am shy, painfully so; and I am deeply private. Those who know me well will immediately recognize the fact of this assertion. Those with whom I am not well acquainted may find it difficult to believe, somewhat at odds with the person they know, a person who is seemingly outgoing, ebullient. All of those things are true. Human beings are complicated creatures, especially when it comes to our interior lives. We know this to be true of ourselves, but we often base our judgment of others only on their outward presentation. When *Willow Weep for Me* was published, a comment that I repeatedly heard—from acquaintances, from audience members at my speaking engagements, and from random people I would meet at social events—was "You don't seem depressed." To this, I would always respond, "What is your image of a person who is experiencing clinical depression? Describe it to me."

When I look in the mirror, what I see is a Black woman who has battled depression her entire life. To be clear: for me, it is no longer a daily battle, not like it was during my teen years and early adulthood. The older I get, the better I have become at self-care, at knowing what triggers an episode of depression and how to lessen its impact or altogether avoid it. This is language that's probably familiar to anyone with a chronic illness. It's the language of someone who has learned how to live without their illness, but knows it can always return, so incorporates activities in their daily routine that, with any luck, will prevent a reoccurrence. Remission and cure are not synonyms. Which is why nobody uses the word "cure" when speaking of mental illness. No matter how well I take care of myself—with meditation, journaling, gratitude practice, exercise, a healthy diet, avoidance of toxic people, proper sleep hygiene, or medication—there is always the possibility that circumstances outside of my control might trigger an episode of depression.

What I mean by "circumstances outside of my control" are overt acts as well as microaggressions of racism and/or misogyny (also known as "misogynoir," when directed toward Black women, who stand at the intersection of two heavily oppressed identities); anti-immigrant sentiments and other forms of xenophobia; physical illness, my own or that of loved ones;

the death of family members, friends, and colleagues; the isolation and other sudden changes brought on by a global pandemic. These are just a few examples. There are an endless number of things that can have a devastating impact on an individual's mental health, incidents over which they are completely powerless.

I was battling depression before I wrote the book; I was battling depression while I wrote the book; and, contrary to what many might imagine, I've battled depression since the publication of the book. I have often been asked whether writing *Willow Weep for Me* made me feel better, whether it had a positive effect on my depression. The answer to that is *yes*. I felt a healing taking place with each word I wrote. By the time the book was published and in the hands of readers, I knew that no matter what, I would win my struggle—against silence.

Zora Neale Hurston wrote: "If you are silent about your pain, they'll kill you and say you enjoyed it." By telling the world about my history of depression, explaining the experiences in my life that might have contributed to the illness, I set aside the stigma of mental illness, particularly the shame that is part and parcel of it, and instead, for the first time in my life, I gave myself grace.

Far too many people who battle against depression suffer in silence, along with the isolation that silence manufactures. I believe this is one of the reasons why clinical depression sometimes leads to suicide; not the only reason, perhaps, but certainly a significant one.

In 1995, while I was writing *Willow Weep for Me*, the singer Phyllis Hyman died by suicide after drinking a deadly cocktail of barbiturate pills and alcohol. She left a note, the initial part of which read, "I'm tired. I'm tired." A few days after I started writing these pages, the 2019 Miss USA and *Extra!* television show correspondent Cheslie Kryst died by suicide after leaping from the twenty-ninth floor of the sixty-story building in which she lived. Before her death, Ms. Kryst posted a photo of herself on the social media site Instagram with a caption that read, "May this day bring you rest and peace."

After each of these tragedies, I listened as people asked, "Why would a woman with so much potential and such a bright future ahead kill herself?" How could a woman with so much talent, beauty, and success be anything but happy? Over and over again, friends of each woman said in printed articles, and on television and radio interviews, "She didn't seem depressed."

Sadly, there are many other Black women who have died by suicide in the last two-and-a-half to three decades, but the deaths of Phyllis Hyman and Cheslie Kyrst were especially heartbreaking because of where I happened to find myself when I heard the news—at a computer, searching for the words to explain to anyone who might care enough to read, to want to know, how insidious and deceptively dangerous depression can be. What words could I possibly write, I wondered, after Phyllis Hyman's death and, again, after Cheslie Kryst's, that will save Black women?

More often than not, the people at highest risk of self-harm are not the ones who speak openly about their depression and allow others to see their vulnerability; rather, it is the individuals who appear sturdy and self-confident, always outgoing and composed; the ones whose pain is shrouded in secrecy, shame, and silence. I know because I have been that person.

———◆———

THOUGH THE SUBTITLE of this book is *A Black Woman's Journey Through Depression*—and though I do, throughout its pages, directly address the topic of race and the role it frequently plays in the (mis)diagnosis and treatment of mental illness—I am realizing now that I merely skimmed the surface of this issue. The racism in America is seething, and, if you are a nonwhite person in this country, its poison is evident in every aspect of your life—nutrition, education, finance, housing and real estate, employment and career, religious and spiritual observance, and, alarmingly, medical care.

In the early days of the pandemic my daughter, Korama, like many other twentysomethings, moved back home. We'd heard news reports of how the COVID virus was attacking the lungs, causing them to swell and then fill with fluid and debris. When the virus kills in this way, it is said to feel like a death by drowning. I ordered a pulse oximeter so we could check our oxygen levels at home. Unlike me, who glances at instructions and then tosses them to the side, my daughter reads them thoroughly.

"Mom," she said, "this doesn't work well on Black people." I stopped what I was doing and read the part of the paper where it explained that because of my skin color, the device may overestimate my oxygen saturation. In other words, I could be at a critically low oxygen level and the device could say that my oxygen saturation is perfect. I was angry, prepared to write that manufacturer a nasty note, when Korama, who'd gone on the Internet to read more about pulse oximetry in general, explained that it isn't just one company or device; the entire technology was created with only white skin in mind. But, she explained, if we wear a white glove while using the pulse oximeter, the reading may be more accurate. Hmm . . .

The COVID crisis really brought the issue of systemic medical racism to the fore. It showed us firsthand that even though illnesses might not discriminate, we live in a world where people do. This affects the care and treatment that others get while they are ill and, in many cases, it can determine whether someone lives or dies.

Every week it seems another Black woman or man is unjustifiably shot and killed by the police. Some critics say it only seems this way because everyone has a cell phone and can capture these incidents on video, and the twenty-four-hour news cycle, as well as social media outlets, broadcast more information than ever before. Whatever the case, it is, to say the least, devastating. Add to that the nationwide increase of crimes based on racial hatred, the fact that gun violence is at an all-time high, and the current attacks on women's bodily autonomy, and Black women's prospects for wellness and joy seem rather bleak.

During a 1961 radio interview, the writer James Baldwin was asked to speak about being Black in America. He said, "To be a Negro in this country and to be relatively conscious is to be in a state of rage . . . almost all of the time—and in one's work. And part of the rage is this: It isn't only what is happening to you. But it's what's happening all around you and all of the time in the face of the most extraordinary and criminal indifference, indifference of most white people in this country, and their ignorance."

So, there is that, too—the public indifference, which often manifests as silence. And the rage in response to that indifference, that silence, often manifests as depression. It is a normal adaptive response. How else is a person supposed to feel when they realize they are an endangered species? How accessible are freedom and joy to a person who knows that no matter what they are doing or not doing—whether they are outside walking or eating or driving or shopping, or at home sleeping in their own bed—they can be executed by an individual in a uniform with a badge and a gun who acts with impunity?

When it becomes clinical, depression is also an illness. If there is a public indifference to our suffering, a public silence in the face of our pain, as well as a private indifference among our intimates that coaxes a private silence, how can we ever heal? In what space are we able to create joy, practice love, be free? In what liminal state?

The greatest opportunity that arose from my depression was learning and embracing self-care. I had never been taught that. Not at home, or at school. Women are so often taught to put the needs and concerns of others first, to be caretakers of everyone else. I had, in fact, been led to believe that prioritizing my own well-being was selfish and self-indulgent. Nothing could be further from the truth. When I learned to respect and value myself, my life started to feel like it had meaning. I started to feel like a part of something larger than myself. "Caring for myself is not self-indulgence," the poet Audre Lorde wrote, "it is self-preservation, and that is an act of political warfare."

Self-care can be defined in myriad ways. What I'm specifically referring to in these pages can be as simple as sleeping and waking up at a reasonable hour, brushing one's teeth and showering daily, exercising regularly, eating food that is healthy, journaling, or reciting affirmations. Self-care is also removing yourself from the proximity of people who cause you harm, emotionally or physically, if you are able. If you are not yet able to do that, then finding the help you need to create a plan to ultimately move yourself to safety. Self-care is finding a therapist and attending sessions every week or twice a week or however regularly the two of you decide is beneficial. Nearly three decades ago, when I first started searching for a therapist, it felt a bit like a scavenger hunt.

Fortunately, therapy is now available everywhere—even via text messaging. This makes it easier to find someone who is a good fit. In addition to talk therapy, there are other forms of therapy. I have always been an avid reader, but had never heard of bibliotherapy, a type of creative arts therapy. In bibliotherapy, the art of storytelling, particularly the narratives of individuals who have had similar experiences to yours, is used to gain perspective, understanding, and, hopefully, healing.

Literature has always been used therapeutically. Much has been written about the inscription above the doors of the library of the Egyptian pharaoh Ramses II, who ruled from 1279 to 1213 BCE: *Healing Place of the Soul*. The term "bibliotherapy," however, was first coined in 1916 by Samuel

McChord Crothers in a satirical essay he wrote for the *Atlantic Monthly* titled "A Literary Clinic."

"I don't care," Crothers wrote in the essay, "whether a book is ancient or modern, whether it is English or German, whether it is in prose or verse, whether it is a history or a collection of essays, whether it is romantic or realistic. I only ask, 'What is its therapeutic value?'"

In 2020, at the start of the pandemic, I decided to try bibliotherapy and even started a popular book club, and I am thrilled that I did. Without that, I don't know how I would have gotten through parts of the pandemic in one piece.

As I found myself watching numerous videos, one right after the other, of a Black person being murdered; reading newspaper articles about white supremacists marching with torches and swastikas; and, hearing about various Black Lives Matter marches and protests, and more Black Lives Matter marches, more Black Lives Matter protests, I realized that it was just too much for me. I started to shut down. I was anxious all the time, unable to fall asleep easily or stay asleep for any meaningful length of time, which made waking and daytime functioning extremely difficult. It was the perfect prelude to a major depressive episode.

I had to remind myself that self-care is an important component of activism. Instead of watching the news and doom-scrolling on the Internet, I started going for walks and making sure I was eating properly. At my suggestion, my friends and I spoke of things other than the ongoing trial of the police officer who'd murdered George Floyd, or the rising COVID death toll, or any other troubling current event. And I started reading.

I read books about the civil rights movement, about the Red Summer, and about a host of other incidents in the history of Black America that offered insight into the political and cultural moment in which I found myself. I read novels, collections of essays, and countless volumes of poetry. I even fell asleep every night while listening to an audiobook.

It wasn't that I was ignoring what was going on or in denial about the nation's state of affairs, but what I had been doing wasn't helping anyone, least of all me. In order to give the best of yourself, you've got to be your best self. I'm a writer; I believe words are majestic and magical, imbued with powers we have not yet begun to understand. So, I started reading and writing. Had I been a visual artist, I most likely would have started painting.

I collect photos of my literary and political heroes that I pin to a corkboard in my office. The photos I prefer are the ones in which they are laughing, the camera having caught them off guard, or the ones in which they are engaged in a leisurely activity, like dancing or hanging out with friends. My favorites are one, by Chester Higgins Jr., of the poets Maya Angelou and Amiri Baraka dancing, and another of Dr. Martin Luther King Jr. and Harry Belafonte cracking up as though they'd just heard the most hilarious joke in the world. Those photographs remind me that time devoted to one's happiness and peace of mind is not wasted. Not at all; quite the opposite. I think this is especially true for Black people, Black women in particular.

——◆——

Laugh as much as possible. You must. Because the world will give you every reason to weep. So as often as possible, you laugh.
—Maya Angelou

IN ORDER TO WRITE this afterword, I sat down and reread *Willow Weep for Me*. It had been years since I'd thought about either the woman I was while writing the book, or the girl I was in the pages of it. Those chapters were long closed. I could barely recognize myself. Ah, but how my heart broke for that deeply depressed and impoverished single mother with no college degree and no employment skills, save typing, and minimal support of any sort from her family. Also, there was one additional impediment that I did not—because I could not—write about at the time: I was an undocumented immigrant, a status that further compounded my problems, eventually making me unemployable and unable to travel. I felt trapped, and my life felt hopeless. There were nights, many nights, when I did not want to wake up the following morning to face the same reality. I was tired of juggling anguish, disappointment, fear, and self-loathing.

"What if I were able to step back in time?" I wondered while reading. "What would I do? What would I change?"

I would tell that terribly unhappy teenage girl, the one who swallowed all those pills because she no longer wanted to live, that one day it would all work out.

But it wasn't just in my teens that I courted death. There were many nights in my twenties and thirties when I sat alone during the still, quiet hours, daring myself to end it all. If I could return to each of those nights, I would whisper in that young woman's ear, "I know you're tired, but please stay. Stay, because even though tomorrow might feel the same, change is indeed happening. There are days in your future that will be different than anything you have ever known. They will be wonderful. Stay, and you will be so happy you did."

But I did stay, even without the intervention or hindsight of my future self. I stayed because I had a baby who then became an infant, a toddler, and an elementary student, then a preteen. It never seemed the appropriate time to make my child, my beautiful blameless daughter, Korama, motherless.

Studies have shown that the age of a child at the time of their separation from a parent—through divorce or death, but particularly maternal loss before the age of eleven—is a major risk factor for future physical and mental health problems, especially depression and anxiety. Additionally, there are studies that point to the high likelihood that suicide is hereditary. When one family member dies by suicide, another one often follows, and shortly after, there is another, and then another. That is because the risk factor in those whose first-degree relative has died by suicide increases by 40–50 percent.

My pregnancy may have been accidental, but the decision to carry to term was a clear and considered choice. I have long been curious about the circumstances of my own birth because I have never felt wanted. Not in actions, not in words, save a perfunctory, "I love you, too," usually said in response to my needy, pleading declaration of love.

I didn't want my child to ever feel that way. While I was

pregnant, I promised that baby growing inside my belly that I would never make her regret my choice to bring her into the world and, more specifically, into my life. I stayed because keeping that promise I made meant more to me than anything, even my own life.

The sections in the memoir about my old Washington, D.C., neighbor and friend, Scott Riley, are haunting. Scott helped me tremendously through several episodes of depression, despite not knowing anything about the illness or really understanding it. He asked questions, withheld judgment, and always led with empathy. I couldn't have asked for a better caretaker.

Ironically, shortly after I left town, Scott started to experience severe episodes of depression. I make mention of this, and his first attempt at suicide, in the final chapter of the book. There were other attempts. He was in treatment with a psychiatrist, the same one I'd worked with while I was living in D.C.

Scott's depression had turned deadly, and he knew it, so he decided to check himself into the psychiatric ward of a local hospital. During the intake process, he was very briefly left unattended, it was only a matter of minutes, but that was enough time for Scott to walk out of the hospital, then down the street to an overpass bridge, where he leapt into the fast-moving city traffic on the street below and died. That was in 1999.

For years, I worried that my other dear friend from that same period, Jade Parsons, would one day die by suicide. We spoke of it often, she and I. She was never fully committed to either living or dying, never sure which one was the solution for her. But they were choices, always there to revisit, if need be . . . until very recently, when Jade promised her sister that she would not take her own life. "I gave her my word," Jade told me during a recent phone conversation. "And I intend to keep it. When you make a promise like that, it's a whole different navigation system." Though she still battles with trauma and mental health challenges, Jade is building a wonderful life for herself. She and her husband have a home in the Carolinas that's filled with love and joy and pets.

Jade balks at such romanticized descriptions. "They never give the full picture," she explains. "It sounds so clean and perfect on paper, but real life is messy." Real life, we both agreed during that conversation, usually happens in the space between the perfect and the awful. There are hard days, even when you are in a good emotional space; just as there are good days, even when you are in a bad emotional space.

I first learned that from Mrs. Patricia Bledsoe, whom I took to calling Mama Bledsoe. Having Jade, who is my peer, and Mama Bledsoe, who was older than my own mother, to speak with openly about my depressions, was a real game-changer. Therapy is one thing, and it's a good thing, but for Black women, community and sisterhood are crucial. To share a space with your peers and aunties, a space in which you can be free to speak your pain, whether it's a body pain or a soul pain, is an act of witness, an act of love—the sort of love that is revolutionary, the sort of love that heals intergenerational wounds, because as Black women, we are more than bone, blood, skin, and hair. We are all who have come before. The memory of their traumas is in our cells, in our dreams, in the languages spoken by our pains, emotional and physical. Jade and Mama Bledsoe offered me that space.

What is important to understand is that it was a space of joy and compassion, confession and empathy and forgiveness. It wasn't a support group with first names only, rituals, and rules. Those groups have their place and purpose. This space that I had with Jade Parsons and Mama Bledsoe, I'd never had that before, but I knew that I could never again be without it in my life.

In 2014, Mama Bledsoe passed away. Until the very end, she battled valiantly against those harsh seasonal episodes of depression she regularly experienced.

Her son, Eugene Bledsoe, passed away in late 2021 at age sixty-four of a sudden cardiac arrest. He and I remained close throughout our entire friendship. After the first fifteen years, during which we spoke pretty much every day, we started easing back our conversations to twice a week, sometimes even once a week.

My friendship with Eugene was one of the most consequential in my life. Through the years, I have often wondered where I would be and what would have become of me had Eugene not entered my life, had he not told me that he believed I was suffering from clinical depression. It wasn't just that he pointed it out; it was that he loved and cared for me like family. That is why I felt safe enough to make the journey from awareness to acceptance, to treatment and then, in time, to wellness. I knew that I wasn't alone.

A few years before Eugene passed away, before the global pandemic hit, he and I had lunch in Manhattan. During that lunch we took a rare trip down memory lane. I had just ordered tea from our server, and I'd asked to please allow the water to hit a rolling boil before serving it to me.

Eugene cracked up. He reminded me that on the day the book proposal for this memoir sold, I had no gas service in my home; it had been disconnected for nonpayment. Heat was not a concern because it was summertime in Southern California. It meant, however, that the stove and oven were useless; also, there was no hot water flowing from the faucets. I could not afford an electric kettle to heat water. I would, instead, fill a glass bowl and then microwave it. That is how I bathed my daughter, who was a toddler then. And I would have to do it right there on the kitchen counter in a yellow plastic bathtub because water boiled in the microwave doesn't take long to turn tepid.

The server returned. He set an empty teacup on a saucer in front of me, and right next to that, a silver gooseneck kettle, steam rising from the spout. "You clean up well," Eugene teased. I smiled, adjusted an imaginary crown on my head, looked at him, and the two of us laughed. It was an inside joke from the very early years of our friendship. Whenever Eugene learned that I hadn't followed up on a lead for a writing assignment, grant, or fellowship he'd suggested I apply for, he wouldn't berate or scold or say anything to make me feel inadequate. He knew it was due to a crisis of confidence, an issue of self-worth. At those times, Eugene would simply remind me of my crown. It was our inside thing, a shorthand between us about this James Baldwin quote: "Our crown has already been bought and paid for. All we have to do is wear it."

THERE IS AN OLD FOLK SONG, "Keep Your Eyes on the Prize," that was popular in the 1950s and '60s during the

American civil rights movement. One of the song's lyrics is, "I got my hand on the gospel plow / wouldn't take nothing for my journey now / keep your eyes on the prize, hold on, hold on." The song is about perseverance, keeping on, despite whatever difficulties and adversities one might face. Dr. Maya Angelou used part of the lyric as the title of her first essay collection, *Wouldn't Take Nothing for My Journey Now*.

Those words perfectly describe how I feel about the life I've led. I am a product of everything that has happened to me—the neglect, the abuses, the betrayals, the poverty, the fears, the friendships, the acts of kindness and generosity, the miracles, the dreams, and the hard work. All of that is what urged, edged, and, sometimes, hurled me forward, helped transform me into a healthy, self-loving, solidly middle-class author with a master of fine arts degree, numerous credits and accolades, and a close, loving relationship with Korama, my wildly intelligent and talented daughter. I am deeply grateful for all the opportunities that I have been given thus far. Life is something special, and I am here, staying, for all of it.

———◆———

Me and you, we got more yesterday than anybody. We need some kind of tomorrow.

—Toni Morrison, *Beloved*

CRITERIA FOR MAJOR DEPRESSION*

Five (or more) of the following symptoms have been present during the same 2-week period and represent a change from previous functioning; at least one of the symptoms is either (1) depressed mood or (2) loss of interest or pleasure.

NOTE: Do not include symptoms that are clearly due to a general medical condition, or mood-incongruent delusions or hallucinations.

1. depressed mood most of the day, nearly every day, as indicated by either subjective report (e.g., feels sad or empty) or observation made by others (e.g., appears tearful). Note: In children or adolescents, can be irritable mood.

2. markedly diminished interest or pleasure in all, or almost all, activities most of the day, nearly every day (as indicated by either subjective account or observation made by others)

3. significant weight loss when not dieting or weight gain (e.g., a change of more than 5% of body weight in a month), or decrease or increase in appetite nearly every day. Note: In children, consider failure to make expected weight gains.

4. insomnia or hypersomnia nearly every day

5. psychomotor agitation or retardation nearly every day (observable by others, not merely subjective feelings of restlessness or being slowed down)

6. fatigue or loss of energy nearly every day

7. feelings of worthlessness or excessive or inappropriate guilt (which may be delusional) nearly every day (not merely self-reproach or guilt about being sick)

8. diminished ability to think or concentrate, or indecisiveness, nearly every day (either by subjective account or as observed by others)

9. recurrent thoughts of death (not just fear of dying), recurrent suicidal ideation without a specific plan, or a suicide attempt or a specific plan for committing suicide

Diagnostic and Statistical Manual of Mental Disorders, Fourth Edition (DSM-IV), Washington, D.C.: American Psychiatric Association, 1994.

CREDITS
